Thinkquiry Toolkit 1

Strategies to Improve Reading Comprehension and Vocabulary Development Across the Content Areas

Julie Meltzer & Dennis Jackson, Editors

The resources and materials in *Thinkquiry Toolkit 1* were developed and field-tested by Public Consulting Group's staff and consultants.

Special thanks to Katanna Conley and

Christine Anderson-Morehouse
Doris Bonneau
Brianne Cloutier
Betty Jordan
BJ Kemper
Mary Ann Liberati

Jennie Marshall
Kevin Perks
Melvina Phillips
Kimberly Schroeter
Pamela Thompson
Roz Weizer
Susan Ziemba

Key support for this work was provided over the past ten years by Nora Kelley and Barbara Hoppe, Elizabeth O'Toole, and Diane Stump.

PCG Education
200 International Drive, Suite 201
Portsmouth, New Hampshire 03801
PublicConsultingGroup.com
pcgeducation@publicconsultinggroup.com

ISBN 978-0-615-40923-8

The *Triple Entry Vocabulary Journal* scenario and the *Save The Last Word for Me* scenario are modified from CCSSO's Adolescent Literacy Toolkit, developed by Public Consulting Group's Center for Resource Management, in partnership with the Council of Chief State School Officers (August 2007). The content was informed by feedback from CCSSO partners and state education officials who participate in CCSSO's Secondary School Redesign Project.

A version of the *Analytic Graphic Organizer* and *Interactive Word Wall* scenario was used in a modified form in the vignette in Appendix A of Irvin, Meltzer, and Duke (2007). Taking action on adolescent literacy: An implementation guide for school leaders. Alexandria, VA: ASCD. We would like to thank Marshalyn Baker for inspiring the development of this scenario.

Front cover Literacy image created with www.wordle.net.

Printed in the United States of America
10 11 12   TT1   1 2 3 4 5 6 7 8 9

Table of Contents

Index of Templates

Index of Classroom Scenarios

Literacy
writing
reading
school
assessment
student
support
development
Adolescent
Leaders
students
strategies
media
area
team
content
Collaborative
instruction
specific
classes
writers
vocabulary

Introduction

Welcome to *Thinkquiry Toolkit 1*, a collection of teacher instructional practices, student learning strategies, and collaborative routines that improve reading comprehension and vocabulary learning in grades 4–12. To be selected as a *Thinkquiry* tool, the practice, strategy, or routine had to be research-based, high impact, and multi-purpose. We have also verified with teachers that each *Thinkquiry* tool works with students in multiple content areas to improve reading and learning.

These tools are tried and true. Our consultants have been working with them for the past 10 years in multiple settings including high schools, career and technical education centers, middle schools, elementary schools, rural schools, urban schools, suburban schools, and digital academies. These tools support the reading comprehension and vocabulary development of honor students, struggling students, apathetic students, and students on grade level. When you teach students the strategies and routines using the *gradual release of responsibility* model, then ask them to use the strategies regularly, match them to your purposes for teaching and learning, and coach them to use them effectively and independently, you—and the students—will be pleasantly surprised by what they are able to accomplish when reading, discussing, analyzing, or creating content-rich text.

Why did we develop *Thinkquiry*?

In 1999, we made a good guess that turned out to be right on target.

We were asked what the next most important issue was going to be in education. That is, what needed to be addressed to ensure that students had the opportunities to be successful in college, in the workplace, and as citizens? Our answer: content area literacy.

We did not mean "basic reading skills"—although these are certainly necessary. We meant the ability to read, write, speak, listen, and think well enough to learn whatever one wanted to learn, to demonstrate that learning, and to transfer that learning to new situations.

The more we researched and worked with students and with teachers, the more we were convinced that the central tenets of this type of literacy were *creative and critical thinking,* and that reading and writing were best understood as *meaning-making* and *problem-solving* processes. Clearly, there were literacy skills that were used across content areas (e.g., activating prior knowledge, questioning). There also seemed to be literacy demands specific to each content area, such as specific types of vocabulary, different types of presentation formats, and various ways of thinking.

We began to compile strategies and approaches that taught students how to read, write, discuss, and think as needed in each content area. Teachers across the country began using these tools with their students in grades 4–12 and gave us feedback as to what worked well, how they used the tools, and the challenges they faced while teaching the strategies. We developed the materials in this *Thinkquiry Toolkit*[1] to provide directions, templates, examples, and scenarios based on teacher requests.

---

[1] *Thinkquiry Toolkit 2* is currently in development and will focus on strategies for strengthening writing across the content areas: writing to learn and writing to communicate. *Thinkquiry Toolkit 3* will focus on strategies students can use to do research and communicate powerfully with and without technology—skills required for success in the 21st century.

The purpose of the teacher instructional practices and collaborative routines included in this Toolkit is to help students develop the skills they need to be excellent readers, learners, and thinkers. The goal of teaching the learning strategies is for students to be able to use the strategies appropriately and independently when reading and learning new content. To accomplish this, the tools must be used regularly across content areas. This is important. If the tools are treated as occasional "activities," they will not work.

Our hope is that a grade level team, a department, a teaching team, or a whole school will take on these instructional practices, student learning strategies, and collaborative routines, teach them to students, and use them regularly. Once students begin using and experiencing the *Thinkquiry* tools regularly across content areas, they will develop confidence and competence as readers, writers, and learners. Isn't that what we want for our students: to be independent learners who can learn effectively even when we are not there to help them?

It comes back to the old adage: by using the *Thinkquiry* teacher instructional practices, student learning strategies, and collaborative routines *you can teach students how to catch fish (learn, read, write, think) not just feed them fish (content).*

Becoming an independent confident learner is required for success in the 21st century. We know that it is possible to teach struggling readers and writers the strategies used by stronger readers, writers, and thinkers. As a teacher, you can use the *Thinkquiry* tools to do this. If students become proficient users of the tools, you will be impressed with how much they are able to accomplish.

Format of the Toolkit

Thinkquiry Toolkit 1 is divided into four sections: **Selecting the Right Tools**, **Laying the Foundation**, **Building New Knowledge**, and **Expanding and Deepening Understanding**. Part 1 describes how to select and prepare to use the right tools. As with construction and painting, knowing how to select the appropriate tools for a given task and prepare the site is critical.

Reading and learning are processes with three distinct phases: *Before*, *during*, and *after*. Parts 2, 3, and 4 of the Toolkit correspond to one of these phases, providing tools that students and teachers can use to develop the habits and skills needed in that phase. Below is a brief overview of the contents of each part of the Toolkit.[2]

Part 1: Selecting the right tools for maximum learning

In Part 1, we provide information that is key to using the *Thinkquiry* tools effectively. The tools are powerful but they have to be carefully selected and explicitly taught for students to use them to their greatest advantage. *We strongly suggest that readers spend time reviewing the concepts in Part 1.* Part 1 includes topics such as:

- Why content teachers are key
- Why strategies and schema matter
- The literacy engagement instruction cycle
- The literacy demands of different content areas
- The connection between vocabulary development and reading comprehension

---

[2] Content about how to support students before, during, and after reading/learning is adapted from CCSSO's *Adolescent Literacy Toolkit*. Available from http://programs.ccsso.org/projects/adolescent_literacy_toolkit/

- The research about vocabulary learning and reading comprehension
- The *gradual release of responsibility* model
- Matching the right tool to the type of text you ask students to read
- Differentiation – what to do when you have students at different reading levels in the same class
- Designing lesson plans that support vocabulary development, improve reading comprehension, and increase content learning

Part 2: Laying the foundation *before* reading/learning

The tools in Part 2 focus on preparing students for content reading and learning by

- Activating prior knowledge by considering what is already known about a content topic.
- Setting purpose and generating questions for learning.
- Previewing to determine how text features, graphs and charts, appendices, and other text structures can contribute to the reader's understanding.
- Making predictions about what might happen, adjusting these predictions as new information is presented, and discarding them when faced with contradictory information.

Part 3: Building new knowledge *during* reading/learning

The tools in Part 3 help learners comprehend content information and construct concepts and relationships by

- Questioning to clarify and deepen understanding.
- Monitoring understanding and using fix-up strategies, such as rereading, reading on, or examining a word more closely.
- Making connections by using information from personal experiences, other texts, and knowledge of world issues to make sense of text.
- Inferring by using prior knowledge to get a deeper understanding of text and making valuable connections with the author's intent when the answer may not be explicitly stated.
- Drawing conclusions and refining them in light of additional information.
- Creating mental images or visualizing.
- Analyzing story structure and informational text structures and using these structures as supports for building meaning.

Part 4: Expanding and deepening understanding *after* reading/learning

The tools in Part 4 help learners reflect on, analyze, and synthesize the content by

- Reflecting on what was read on personal, emotional, and cognitive levels.
- Reviewing information, ideas, relationships, and applications to real life by rereading, summarizing, and discussing with others.
- Summarizing what was read and learned.
- Synthesizing by combining ideas and information within and across texts.
- Presenting concepts learned through the informal and formal written and spoken word, including small group classroom venues and authentic audiences.

Each section's *Thinkquiry* tools are listed in the section introduction. The tools are coded to show when use of them would be most effective, i.e., before, during or after reading/learning. Note that many of the *Thinkquiry* tools can be used to support student learning at more than one phase of the reading process.

How and when you and your students use the tools will depend on your teaching and learning goals, the needs of your students and the specific demands of the text or content being read or learned.

The Tools of the Toolkit

Parts 2, 3 and 4 of the Toolkit describe three types of tools: student learning strategies, collaborative routines, and teacher instructional practices.

Student learning strategies are strategies that we want students to be able to use independently in school and beyond. These strategies have the capacity to improve students' literacy habits and skills with ongoing use. For example, when students go to college or into the workforce, we want them to be able to use **Coding/Comprehension Monitoring**, **Two-Column Notetaking**, or **Sum It Up** strategies if these would be helpful to the task at hand.

Collaborative routines support the social nature of literacy and learning by providing protocols for pair and group work. These are designed to help students use one another as a resource to move successfully through the three phases of reading and learning. Collaborative routines shift the responsibility for learning to students and help students to improve their reading comprehension and vocabulary development when regularly engaged as part of content teaching and learning.

Teacher instructional practices are approaches that teachers can use to support all students to develop the reading, vocabulary learning, and thinking skills of strong readers, writers, and thinkers.

Each tool is described with steps for implementation and tips for how to deepen student learning or maximize effectiveness. Templates are provided where applicable. Then, for each tool, there is a set of examples of what the tool might look like "in action" in grades 4–12 in various content areas. Finally, at the end of each section, there are more extended classroom scenarios.

Different populations can use *Thinkquiry Toolkit 1* to support students' content literacy development.

- *Individual teachers* of students in grades 4–12 can use the *Thinkquiry Toolkit* to improve their students' reading, writing, vocabulary development, and content learning.

- *Professional learning communities, grade level teams, teaching teams or departments* can use the Toolkit by discussing student literacy needs and selecting strategies, collaborative routines or instructional practices that address specific learning goals. Then teachers can try the approach in their classrooms. When they next meet, they can discuss how they used the strategy, routine or practice, how students responded, and how they would improve their instructional use of the tool next time. Student work resulting from use of the tool could be examined to better understand the impact of the tool on reading and learning.

- *School literacy leadership teams, departments, grade level teams, or teaching teams* can select a common set of *Thinkquiry* strategies to teach students, thereby developing a set of common experiences and language for talking about literacy and learning. Students would see the applicability of the tools across content areas and strengthen their literacy habits and skills.

We hope that you find *Thinkquiry Toolkit 1* to be helpful in supporting your efforts to improve students' vocabulary development, reading comprehension, and learning across the content areas.

Julie Meltzer and Dennis Jackson, October 2010

Literacy
writing
reading
student
students
Leaders
support
Adolescent
development
strategies
assessment
media
team
specific
instruction
classes
writers

Part 1: Selecting the Right Tools

Part 1: Selecting the Right Tools

What is the best time to use analytic graphic organizers?

Why does the Toolkit focus on vocabulary and reading comprehension at the same time?

What can I do when I have some students who read just fine and others in the same class who can't read the textbook?

I am a content teacher – am I really expected to work on reading comprehension?

I use instructional strategies that work just fine – why should I use the ones in this Toolkit?

Teachers across the country have asked these and many other questions related to content reading and learning. Before we get to the sections of the Toolkit that describe and provide examples of the actual tools, we think it is important to address many of the issues that concern math, science, social studies and English language arts teachers—as well as their colleagues who teach foreign language, technical arts, fine arts, business, health, music and other subject areas. It is easy to "mandate" that all content area teachers focus on improving reading comprehension and vocabulary development. It is harder to provide practical guidelines for how teachers might do that in ways that increase student engagement and content learning. In this section of the Toolkit, we try to do just that. These are the types of tips and guidelines that teachers we have worked with find most useful.

We begin with a discussion of why content area teachers are the ones who need to use the *Thinkquiry* tools —why this is not only desirable, but necessary. We start here because we think that teachers have a right to know why their use of these tools can be critical to student success.

Content teachers are key to supporting students to become better readers, writers, and thinkers

Why do all content area teachers need to actively support the ongoing literacy development of their students?

We are asked this question all the time. After all, you signed on to teach math or science or art—not reading. However, it is critical that convince you to take this on as a core aspect of teaching and learning in your content area is critical.

It is important that you understand the importance of your role in strengthening students as readers, writers, and learners. Without your help in this area, many of your students will falter. And that means that they will not learn the content you want them to learn.

> The purpose of the Thinkquiry 1 Toolkit is to provide you with the tools to support students to become stronger readers, writers, and thinkers about the content that you want them to learn.

Here are the four critical reasons why YOU need to become even more effective at developing students' literacy abilities as an integral part of teaching and learning in your content area—and why, collectively, content area teachers need to provide the bulk of the support to students for ongoing content literacy development (Irvin, Meltzer, & Dukes, 2007).

1. You know your content.
2. You know the reading, writing, speaking, and thinking demands of the content you teach.
3. You have the access and the opportunity—you see students regularly.

4. You and your colleagues have the collective power to make a real difference in the amount of content reading and writing students do—and the amount and quality of supportive instruction they receive.

The purpose of the *Thinkquiry 1 Toolkit* is to provide you with the tools—the teacher practices, student learning strategies and collaborative routines—that you can use to support students to become stronger readers, writers, and thinkers about the content that you want them to learn.

Why *Thinkquiry* tools work with students in grades 4–12

The role of motivation and engagement in literacy and learning

As students attend school through the upper grades, many studies suggest that students in general, and particularly boys, read less. When asked why, students indicate many reasons including lack of interest in the assigned reading, lack of confidence in their own abilities as readers, and difficulty understanding the text (whether print or electronic, literary or nonfiction; whether the information is presented primarily through words or visuals). *Thinkquiry* tools are designed to help students increase their confidence in reading text, their proficiency in reading, as well as their engagement with the text. When teachers combine the tools with interesting reading and writing assignments, authentic reasons to read and write, and opportunities to engage in meaningful inquiry about a topic—student engagement typically soars.

> When you combine *Thinkquiry* tools with interesting reading and writing assignments, authentic reasons to read and write, and opportunities to engage in meaningful inquiry about a topic—student engagement typically soars.

It is also true that students are less willing to engage with the material if they have a lack of accessible appropriate vocabulary they can use when reading, writing, or presenting on a subject. If someone does not understand "the language," it is much harder to engage in discussion or to have any deep sense of what is being discussed or read about. And it turns out that when the brain is not able to make sense of a situation, it disengages, making it hard to learn from text. Building background knowledge along with teaching and practicing the use of academic, technical, and conceptual vocabulary helps build confidence that the assigned reading and learning is, in fact, doable. Thus, the *Thinkquiry* tools that specifically assist with vocabulary development can have a positive effect on getting students to engage with the text.

Reading about a topic independently and understanding what was read is a key career, college, and citizenship skill. However, many teachers just figure that students will not read the assigned reading. Instead of engaging students with the reading, teacher might enable students not to read by telling them the main points covered by the text. Many upper elementary, middle, and high school teachers express frustration about "not knowing how to get students to read." Again, the *Thinkquiry* tools—especially the collaborative routines—can help. Teachers are often impressed with how engaged students become when using the collaborative routines to work through text with other students.

It is impossible to improve students' skills as readers, writers, and thinkers when they refuse to engage with text. In general, people do not improve their skills when they refuse to practice or use the skills they have. Therefore, it is important for all teachers to work with students in ways that support them to regularly read, write, and think critically and creatively in response to what they have read or learned. Using the *Thinkquiry* tools to help students engage with reading—print or online—and learning, can be very helpful. In addition, the more students use the *Thinkquiry* strategies, the more comfortable they become with using them—resulting in a more productive use of the strategies by students.

Strategies and schema matter!

Strategies. A good strategy enables someone to effectively and efficiently make meaning of a task so that a goal can be accomplished. Selecting the right strategy can make the difference between not completing a task, completing a task at a minimal level of quality, and completing a task well.

Selecting the right strategy requires that you understand what the task requires (purpose) and that you know a variety of strategies you might use to accomplish the task. Using a strategy means that you know the strategy and are confident that you can use it well enough to accomplish task. For example, if you know how to skim and scan and you know how to take good notes, you will be able to read a large amount of material in a short amount of time in order to brief your supervisor on the pros and cons of a new textbook series. If, on the other hand, you cannot skim and scan well and are not able to select the important points to capture in your notes, you will not be able to complete the task.

Schema. Schema is the background knowledge or prior knowledge related to the task you are being asked to do. It is much easier to read a technical article about rare breeds of sheepdogs if you know something about sheep herding and something about dog breeding. If you know about neither of these, it will be a lot harder to understand what you are reading and you may end up confused or unable to explain more than the gist of the article to someone else.

But just knowing a set of facts that you can repeat on a test is not "schema." Teaching for understanding requires that we shift teaching in all content areas from skipping from topic to topic to having students understand why something is important to know. The key is supporting students to make connections between what is being learned with what has been studied previously, while building conceptual understanding and looking for patterns. In fact, this type of learning is what distinguishes novices from experts or those able to develop expertise. Teachers can seed new learning with key information, then ask students to recall what they already know (or think they know!), ask what they want to know about the topic or concept, and, after reading and learning, ask them to reflect on what has been learned and what questions they now have (see, for example, the teacher practice **KWL Plus** in Part 2 of this Toolkit).

> The key is supporting students to make connections between what is being learned with what has been studied previously while building conceptual understanding and looking for patterns.

Let's say you have planned to teach a unit on photosynthesis or the Civil War or the stock market or the genre of biography or memoir. In all of these cases, to build schema and conceptual knowledge will require planning how to layer learning and support students to become engaged with multiple types of text (prose, electronic, primary sources, visual, narrative, tables and graphs, numeric). And in all cases, the *Thinkquiry* tools can help by providing students with strategies they can use as readers and learners to make meaning of the material.

So how are strategies different from activities? And why are they so important when it comes to reading and vocabulary development?

Imagine that you have been away on vacation for the past week. When you return, there is a pile of mail. How do you deal with the mail most efficiently? You probably sort it quickly into piles. Perhaps your categories include junk mail, bills, personal mail, and catalogues or magazines that you want to save to read later.

Sorting is a *strategy* to deal effectively with the challenge of a pile of mail. But you did not sort the mail by color or size. You sorted by categories that you knew from prior experience would be useful to you. That is, you matched the *strategy* of sorting with the *purpose* of the task: handling the mail efficiently. From prior knowledge and experience of getting and opening mail, you recognize most types of mail and understand which types will likely be of interest to you. In other words, you have a *schema* for mail, an internal experience map that tells you how it is best to sort in order to accomplish your goal. If you do not have a good schema and a good strategy, you would have to open up and read every piece of mail and decide what to do with it. This would take a very long time. If you were a poor reader—in addition to having no background knowledge and no strategy to handle the task—you might give up.

> Examples of cross-content area literacy demands include activating prior knowledge, setting purpose for reading, clarifying, questioning, predicting, summarizing, visualizing, deductive, and inductive thinking, brainstorming, and responding.

Now let's apply this to reading comprehension and vocabulary development. If you have strategies for reading, you can match your reading speed and approach to your purpose for reading. If you know how and when it is helpful to skim and scan, summarize, code, take notes, then you do not have to try to remember each word every time you read a new text. If you have strategies for concept development, learning technical vocabulary, and remembering academic terms, you do not have to try to memorize words and definitions. *That is why strategies and schema matter.*

Pulling it all together: The Literacy Engagement and Instruction Cycle

Engagement and instruction are not an "either-or" proposition. Both are essential when it comes to improving student literacy and learning. If students are interested in what they are learning, but lack skills to be independent readers, writers and thinkers, then they are completely dependent on the teacher to learn. If students have skills but are disengaged as readers and learners, their skills might atrophy or they might lie dormant and teachers have no opportunity to coach them to higher levels of proficiency. You may not know if students can read if they do not read. All you know is that they refuse to read.

The Literacy Engagement and Instruction Cycle

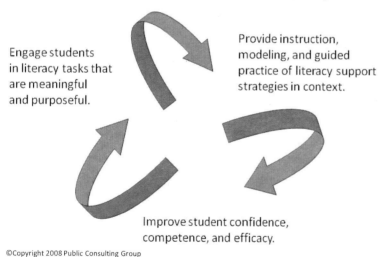

Engage students in literacy tasks that are meaningful and purposeful.

Provide instruction, modeling, and guided practice of literacy support strategies in context.

Improve student confidence, competence, and efficacy.

©Copyright 2008 Public Consulting Group

It might be helpful to think of the *Literacy Engagement and Instruction Cycle* as a coaching cycle. If we can get students on the field to play, we can coach them to greater success. If they feel successful, they are willing to continue playing. If they continue to play, we can continue to coach.

Most adolescents like to argue, make their own choices, interact with one another, set and meet goals, and do things for real reasons. The *Thinkquiry* tools take these dispositions and use them to engage students with print and electronic text. Instead of working against the natural inclinations of teenagers, the *Thinkquiry* tools use students' natural dispositions and help teachers get students to read, write, and think more deeply and with greater comprehension.

Electronic Text and the Use of _Thinkquiry_ Tools

We know that many students will pay more attention and work harder if technology and media are involved. In addition, the sheer availability of the vast repository of accessible information and text on the Internet and open educational resources means that students—and their teachers—now have access to an amazing array of new resources that were previously inaccessible (e.g., museum archives, current health information, up-to-date statistics, primary sources, scientific data of various types). This increases opportunity to learn for everyone. We suggest that you build vocabulary and reading comprehension using technology and media where appropriate. Note that skillful use of electronic text and media may require additional instruction if they are to be maximized in the context of teaching and learning.[3] For example, most students need instruction on how to assess bias, search for relevant information, read hypertext in a meaningful way, understand new online text structures, and evaluate source credibility.

> Instead of working against the natural inclinations of teenagers, the Thinkquiry tools use students' natural dispositions and help teachers motivate students to read, write, and think more deeply and with greater comprehension.

However, it is critical to realize that many of the _Thinkquiry_ reading comprehension and vocabulary tools are, in fact, not only applicable, but important to use when working with electronic texts. Certainly learning how to manage the information glut is a challenge. On a basic level, however, many of the same rules apply when reading electronic text as with print text: you need to be able to make meaning of what you read, you need to practice reading multiple genres, you need to understand the vocabulary, and you need to be able to combine text and vocabulary to deepen and extend understanding.

Technology can also assist students when using the strategies. Some examples include marking or coding online text using color highlighting or use of comments, using electronic templates when completing graphic organizers, posting quick writes to a blog site, or using a wiki when completing group summarizing. Each of these uses of technology can help students record individual or collaborative thinking, make editing and revising and brainstorming easier, and increase students' active engagement when working to make meaning of print or electronic text.

The literacy demands of different content areas

Content literacy is about

- How, why, and what you read and write in a particular content area.
- How and why you speak and present in a given content area.
- The types of thinking required by a specific discipline.
- Applicable vocabulary, formats, text structures, and discourse elements (how you talk about specific content).

Students need to strategically read, write, speak, listen, present, and think across content areas. Of course, the specifics of how you do these vary according each discipline. Examples of across content area literacy demands include activating prior knowledge, setting purpose for reading, clarifying, questioning, predicting, summarizing, visualizing, deductive and inductive thinking, brainstorming, and responding.

---

[3] This is the focus of Thinkquiry Toolkit 3.

There are also specific ways of reading, writing, speaking, and listening, presenting, and thinking within each discipline that are more applicable to some disciplines as opposed to others. Examples include rules of evidence, text types and structures, presentation formats, conceptual vocabulary, and technical vocabulary.

> Vocabulary development is an integral part of content learning and is critical when students are asked to read and write about and discuss specific topics.

Reflect on how successful students read, write, talk about content, and think in the content area you teach. However, many students need tools, strategies, and guided practice to become skilled readers, writers, and thinkers in different content areas. Look at the descriptions below, one for each of the four core content areas. As you read, think about the ways that you help students get better at reading and writing and vocabulary learning given the specific demands of your content area.

Note: Although you may not teach one of the content areas below, chances are the discipline you teach has some of the literacy demands mentioned and may have others as well.

Mathematics

Mathematics is heavily dependent on critical thinking, vocabulary and concept development, and the ability to learn from dense concise text. However, math teachers may not know how to support literacy development. The text formats in the math classroom include word problems, textbooks, proofs, articles, graphs, and charts. Mathematical language usage requires an understanding of operations, terminology that has precise meaning, and relevant conceptual vocabulary. Mathematical writing includes being able to write succinctly and clearly various types of text: problem write-ups, manuals, proofs, statistical analysis, response to problematic situations, notes combining symbols and text, and directions for solving problems and explanations.

Sample literacy tasks for mathematics students

- Read dense explanatory text to better understand processes
- Grasp abstract concepts and translate them into symbols
- Distinguish and describe patterns
- Decode words as well as numeric and non-numeric symbols
- Translate words into problems and problems into words
- Use journals to write about and examine ideas and reflect on solutions
- Compare and contrast key concepts, record logic and proofs, and present solutions to multi-step problems in writing

Science

Science is heavily dependent on reading and research skills, critical thinking and vocabulary and concept development. However, science teachers may not know how to support literacy development. Success in the science classroom requires skilled reading, skimming and scanning, and interpretation of a wide variety of genres and formats including articles, lab reports, textbooks, informational websites, graphs, charts, tables, and complex diagrams. Students use focused language in the study of science including process words, terminology with precise meanings, and conceptual vocabulary. Types of writing include lab reports, analytical essays, notes from text, demonstration, film and lecture, I-search and research projects, observational and procedural notes, summaries, and evidence-based conclusions. Literacy and learning skills are especially critical in the area of science because scientific knowledge is evolving so rapidly and students must constantly learn and evaluate new information and make connections to what they already know.

Sample literacy tasks required of science students

- Compare and contrast concepts and ideas

- Read concept-dense text accompanied by tables, graphs and diagrams
- Analyze and present data
- Write careful and precise observations
- Form hypotheses and draw conclusions
- Understand how the specifics of a particular process or system relate to the "bigger picture"
- Determine the relative importance and accuracy of information
- Write about findings in learning logs or as part of lab report conclusions

Social Studies/History

Social Studies/History is heavily dependent on reading, critical thinking, vocabulary, and concept development and writing. However, social studies teachers may not know how to support literacy development. When studying history and government, students need to be able to read and make sense of information from a wide variety of text formats including primary sources, textbooks, articles, nonfiction texts, maps, historical photographs, government documents, regulations, biography, graphs, charts, and artifacts. When discussing issues in history, students need to understand concepts and how they translate across settings and periods. They need to be able to verbally summarize and debate, taking and defending a point of view. They need to be competent writers who can produce analytical essays, opinion essays, I-search and research projects, summaries, and evidence-based conclusions.

Sample literacy tasks required of social studies/history students

- Sequence and make connections between historical events
- Understand text structures and features
- Evaluate sources
- Recognize issues and trends in context
- Engage in reflective inquiry through reading and writing
- Recognize and write about cause-and-effect relationships
- Distinguish between, and write about, fact versus opinion

English Language Arts

English language arts is heavily dependent on reading and writing. However, English language arts teachers may not know how to support literacy development, especially in the area of reading. Literary genres and formats—the poem, essay, short story, play, biography, memoir, novel, and letters—require a wide variety of reading approaches and skills. Language usage includes grammar, technical, and conceptual vocabulary related to the study of literature. Types of writing include narrative, persuasive and expository.

Sample literacy tasks for English language arts students

- Articulate thinking orally and in writing for various audiences
- Understand mechanical standards and rhetorical techniques
- Employ context clues
- Recognize literary devices
- Understand how to read different literary genres
- Develop fluency with the use of the writing process to generate different types of writing
- Use the reading/writing connection to persuade, learn, inform, and evoke feelings

As you can see, these skills are not for the fainthearted. Nevertheless, they can be taught using the *Thinkquiry* tools and the *gradual release of responsibility model* (see page 17). Note: *Thinkquiry Toolkit 1* has a number of summarizing strategies and note-taking strategies that will be helpful to students as they read and create text. *Thinkquiry Toolkit 2* will specifically focus on how to develop students as writers across and within content areas.

The connection between vocabulary development and reading comprehension

Vocabulary development is an integral part of content learning and is critical when students are asked to read and write about and discuss specific topics. If students do not know many of the words in a text, it is difficult to understand the big concepts, differentiate between terms, and communicate understanding. Vocabulary development, therefore, must be taught in the context of the content being learned. Students need strategies to learn new vocabulary as well as opportunities to interact with new vocabulary multiple times in multiple ways. When teachers use a variety of approaches to teach vocabulary, they notice that reading comprehension improves, as does the quality of student discussion and written work.

Vocabulary is a critical element in three aspects of reading comprehension.

1. Vocabulary allows the learner to make connections to prior knowledge, develop background knowledge, and preview the content of the material they will read.

2. Knowing the words they will encounter—and actively working to learn the meaning of unfamiliar words while reading—assists readers in the understanding the text. When students understand 75–90% of the words they are reading, comprehension is typically adequate. If they understand less than ¾ of the words that carry meaning in the text, it is difficult for students to make much sense of the text.

3. Developing an understanding of words needed to discuss and write about a topic allows students to think and reflect on the topic, make connections, summarize, and draw conclusions. Students cannot be reflective about the content they are learning if they cannot use the words associated with the content accurately and confidently. Actively working with the content that was read creates new insights, allow students to develop robust understanding and supports students as they build new knowledge – all critical elements of improving reading comprehension.

There are three types of words that students need to learn when engaged in a unit of study.

- Key concepts (e.g., *renewable energy, democracy, exponential, character flaw*)
- Technical vocabulary (e.g., *fuel cell, ballot, denominator, foreshadowing*)
- Academic vocabulary (e.g., *analyze, compute, summarize, evidence*)

An additional issue for vocabulary learning is "multiple meaning words." These are often common words that have very different meanings in different content areas. For example, think about what is meant by the word *power* in a mathematical equation vs. in the study of electricity in science vs. the power of the government in social studies or the power of a character in a novel. Other words like this include: *force, benign, rupture, static, dependent, root*. There are many more. The challenge is that students may have one definition in their mind and take that to different units of study throughout the course of days or weeks. For many students, especially English learners and students who are not avid readers or viewers of television shows such as those found on the Discovery Channel, inadvertent confusion can be the result. Spending a few minutes to quickly clarify the meaning of a common word being used in a specific content context is always worth the time!

You will want to use different strategies and approaches depending on the types of words that students need to learn and the level of understanding that students need to have with the specific words. Students also need to develop strategies for learning unfamiliar terms—strategies they can take with them into college and the workplace where learning and remembering new words remain a lifelong endeavor. Because of the symbiotic relationship between vocabulary development and reading comprehension, you will find it productive to focus students' attention to words *before*, *during*, and *after* reading.

The chart below lists the four vocabulary learning challenges discussed earlier and specific *Thinkquiry* tools that can be used to address them.

Vocabulary learning challenge	*Thinkquiry* tools that can be used
Developing conceptual understanding	Frayer Models, Concept Maps; Word Sorts; list-group-label
Learning and remembering technical words	Interactive Word Walls; Triple-Entry Vocabulary Journals; Semantic Feature Analysis; Knowledge Rating Guides
Learning and remembering academic vocabulary	Word Analysis; Interactive Word Walls; Frayer Models
Multiple meaning words	Knowledge Rating Guides; Word Analysis

Knowing the words, however, is only one aspect of reading comprehension. Once students understand basic concepts and definitions of the word relevant to the content being studied, they then have to be able to make sense of text about that content. This involves more than just decoding the words and understanding literal meaning. According to Elaine McEwan's (2001) synthesis of the research, skilled readers are able to do the following on their own as needed with a variety of types of text.

- Activate prior knowledge
- Make text-based inferences
- Monitor comprehension
- Clarify understanding
- Question the text
- Search for and select pertinent information
- Summarize understanding
- Visualize when reading
- Organize content

You can use the *Thinkquiry* tools to help struggling readers be able to develop and use these same skills with grade level texts. You can use the same tools to help average and above average readers apply these skills to increasingly complex text. We suggest that you review the suggested student strategies and teacher practices in each of the next sections of the Toolkit. Pay special attention to the collaborative routines that are described to support students before, during, and after reading. These are powerful scaffolding techniques that work for all levels of readers and put the responsibility for learning and making meaning of text where it belongs—on the students.

Being able to independently read and understand complex text is highly correlated to being successful in college and the workplace (ACT, 2006). It is also a critical skill for participating as an active citizen in the 21st century. Using the *Thinkquiry* tools frequently in your classroom will support students to improve vocabulary learning and reading comprehension—an educational gift that will keep on giving.

Overview of the research about vocabulary development and reading comprehension

Below is a brief summary of recent research[4] in the area of vocabulary development and reading comprehension. The summary highlights the key ideas that teachers will want to consider when planning and facilitating literacy-rich lessons and units that simultaneously increase content learning.

> Spending a few minutes to quickly clarify the meaning of a common word being used in a specific content context is always worth the time!

Thinkquiry tools specifically address what the research has found to be effective practice in these areas. You may want to review the classroom scenarios at the end of Parts 2, 3, and 4 of the Toolkit to see what these tools look like "in action" when used effectively. If you are interested in reading further about the research related to these key ideas and how they can be used in the upper elementary, middle, and high school classroom, references can be found in the Related Resources section of the Toolkit.[5]

Vocabulary Development Research

Direct explicit instruction. Direct explicit instruction in vocabulary and learning from context are important. Effective instruction includes description rather than definitions and word recognition through multiple interactions.

Strategies. Effective strategies include use of linguistic and nonlinguistic representations; gradual shaping of word meanings through multiple exposure; teaching and using word parts; using different types of instruction for different types of words; students' interaction with words; games; and a focus on academic terms.

Multiple interactions. Repetition and rich support, such as inferring vocabulary meanings from context rather than being given the definition, are essential for increasing vocabulary.

Active engagement. Vocabulary learning should entail active engagement in learning tasks. Teach students to be independent word learners who know how to seek specific word meanings, appreciate multiple meanings of words, and enjoy using new words.

Reading Comprehension Research

Instructional considerations include

Time. Time spent reading and writing helps improve those skills.

Use of strategies. Particular literacy strategies—when explicitly taught, modeled, and practiced before, during, or after reading—enhance the ability of secondary students to read and write to learn across the content areas. Over 200 studies of comprehension strategy instruction, fourth grade and above, found evidence for the efficacy of comprehension monitoring, cooperative learning graphic organizers, story structure, question generating, question answering, summarization, and the use of multiple strategies.

---

[4] For specific research citations, please refer to the References section in the back of this book.

[5] You may also want to reference the *Time to Act* (2009) report issued by the Carnegie Corporation of New York.

Keys to improved reading comprehension include:

Meaningful context. Literacy skills and strategies should be taught in context, not in isolation nor as "skills and drills" worksheets often advocated for remediation.

Cross-content literacy. Content area teachers include modeling and literacy instructions as part of content teaching and learning so students read and write like subject area experts.

Text-based collaborative learning. Instead of general classroom discussion, specific analysis of text with students who have a wide range of abilities.

Use of diverse text. Students are provided with appropriately leveled, diverse texts that present a wide range of topics including texts that connect to students' cultural, linguistic, and demographic backgrounds.

Tips for using the *Thinkquiry* tools in your classroom

Now that you have a sense of how important you are in supporting students to be readers, writers and thinkers and a sense of why and how the *Thinkquiry* tools might be helpful, you need to understand that teaching the strategies and collaborative routines is different than assigning them. In this section, we suggest a number of things to think about when you are planning to integrate the *Thinkquiry* tools into your content instruction on a regular basis.

Use the *gradual release of responsibility* model to teach *Thinkquiry* strategies effectively

In order for the *Thinkquiry* tools to be effective, the research suggests that they should be introduced and taught using the *gradual release of responsibility* model.

This model suggests that teaching students how to use a *Thinkquiry* strategy is similar to how a coach supports an athlete to improve his or her technique. A coach demonstrates (models), explains (explicitly describes and provides tips for how to approach the task), guides practice, and then asks the athlete to try the skill independently, providing feedback until the skill is mastered. This same *gradual release of responsibility* model is helpful to use when teaching students a new learning strategy or collaborative routine. How often do you model and coach how to read and write in your content area? It is important to remember that students *may not know how to do this.*

> *Teaching* Thinkquiry strategies and collaborative routines is different from *assigning* them.

Learning a new skill takes time and practice. To successfully teach students a strategy or collaborative routine from *Thinkquiry Toolkit 1*, you can use the five steps in the *gradual release of responsibility* model.

1. **Pre-assessment** – Think about what types of literacy habits and skills are necessary to be successful on the assigned task and the level of support that students will need. Then select an appropriate *Thinkquiry* strategy, collaborative routine or instructional practice to use with students. Before teaching students how to use the tool, check to see if students know the approach, if they have done it in the past, etc.

2. **Explicit instruction and modeling** – Provide explicit directions and model how to use the strategy or do the collaborative routine. Clarify expectations for quality and suggest tips for successful completion of a task using the approach.

3. **Guided practice** – Ask students to practice the strategy in pairs or small groups and provide ample feedback along the way so that students know whether they are on track or not. Ask the students

to reflect on how the strategy, collaborative routine or instructional support is affecting their reading and learning.

4. **Independent practice** – Ask students to practice the approach on their own with similar content and levels of challenge to what has been practiced with others. Be sure to provide feedback.

5. **Independent application and transfer** – Ask students to apply the strategy or collaborative routine to other situations and contexts.

> What we often forget is that *teaching* is required to teach students how to read, write, and think about the content. *Mere exposure* to the content itself is no guarantee these skills will develop.

Many teachers ask what we mean by "modeling" in Step 2 above. Modeling means actually demonstrating how you go about completing a task using the same strategy you are teaching the students. Thinking aloud is a great way to model how to use a strategy for students. (Note: you may want to refer to the description of the **Think-Aloud** teacher practice in Part 3 of the Toolkit). Because reading is an "invisible" activity, thinking aloud as you complete a reading or learning task provides students with an understanding of approaches they can use. Below are some tips for modeling.

1. Plan
   - What meaning do you want students to construct from the content?
   - What reading comprehension or vocabulary strategy do you want students to learn and use?
2. Identify where you might pause during the passage to "think aloud" for your students.
   - Think aloud about your own experiences related to both the content and the strategy.
   - Take what you know implicitly and make it explicit for students.
3. Mark the pauses with a sticky-note with a short notation of what you'll say.
4. Explicitly explain the **Think-Aloud** strategy before using it.
   - Tell students what strategy you will model, why it helps, and when to use it.
   - Explain that you'll show them what's going on inside your head to construct meaning.
5. Read the text with the students as you do the **Think-Aloud**.
   - Give students a copy of the text to follow along or put the text on an overhead projector so they can visually follow along.
   - Model the chosen thinking tasks by stopping to articulate what's going on in your head.

For example, if you were going to model the **Coding** strategy (see Part 3 of the Toolkit) you would read the text with the students as you complete a **Think-Aloud**, showing how you think about what to code and the decisions you make about which code to use with a particular passage.

Matching the right *Thinkquiry* tool to the type of text you ask students to read

One of the most difficult things for some content teachers to do is finding ways to help students read and comprehend difficult texts. "I'm not a reading teacher," you may lament as you watch your students struggle. This may be the case, but just as a music teacher teaches a student to read music, a physician teaches an intern to read an X-Ray, and a sailor teaches an apprentice to read the night sky, content teachers are the ones with the content expertise to teach students how to read content-specific materials.

The key to doing this successfully lies in asking, and answering, three questions about a text: 1. What is my learning goal?; 2. What about this text might be difficult for my students?; 3. What strategies or tools are best suited to address the challenges this text presents?

1. What is my learning goal?

The first step is developing a clear sense of what you want students to learn or do with the text. Teachers often identify a content learning goal first. For example:

- I want my students to read the chapter to learn what happened during the Second Continental Congress.
- I want my students to read the handout and understand the difference between erosion and weathering.
- My students need to know the different ways to solve quadratic equations that are explained at the beginning of Chapter 8.

These are reasons you might have for students to read specific content area text and, hopefully, the information that you want them to gain from the text will be extended and applied in other ways during the unit of study. Often, however, there are additional learning goals associated with the academic learning and literacy skills you want students to develop. When these are fully identified, it makes it clear where you can productively use *Thinkquiry* tools.

For example, when reading the same texts as above, you probably also want your students to be able to:

- Connect events in our nation's past to conflicts today
  Thinkquiry tools that might be helpful: **Discussion Web, Coding/Comprehension Monitoring,** Venn diagram **Analytic Graphic Organizer, Save the Last Word for Me**
- Compare and contrast two natural processes
  Thinkquiry tools that might be helpful: **Group Summarizing, Jigsaw, Discussion Web, Coding/ Comprehension Monitoring, Picture This!**
- Select the most appropriate problem solving approach for a given context
  Thinkquiry tools that might be helpful: **Semantic Feature Analysis, Five-Step Problem Solving Organizer**

Chances are that some of your students would have difficulty performing these actions with the content they read about. They would need to be taught how to do this as they work with the text. That is where use of the *Thinkquiry* tools comes in.

Considering the academic learning or literacy skills you're trying to teach often suggests how best to approach a text. This makes sense because these academic skills often correspond to the types of thinking teachers understand are most important in their content area. For example, history buffs often talk about how much we can learn about the present by examining the past. In science, classification, close observation, comparison and contrast—these are tools of the trade. Math instructors look to

> In order to scaffold students to read effectively, it is critical to try to look at the text as an outsider and to analyze its cognitive demands.

mathematics as way to help students learn to solve problems. What we often forget is that *teaching is required* to teach students *how* to read, write, and think about the content. Mere exposure to the content itself is no guarantee these skills will develop. Often, the difficulty lies in the familiarity that content teachers have with the cognitive demands of their own content. For example, as a science teacher, you may be so comfortable with what it means to read like a scientist that this is second nature to you. Because reading scientific content without difficulty is commonplace for you, is it becomes particularly difficult to articulate the processes you use to process text so you can model how to do this for your students. In order to scaffold students to read effectively, it is critical, then, to try to look at the text as an outsider and to analyze its cognitive demands.

2. What about this text might be difficult for students?

Note: When you read this next section, you may want to refer to a specific text you will be asking students to read in the near future.

There are several things to consider when you're thinking about what might make a text difficult for students. Fisher, Frey, and Lapp (2009) define four categories.

- Comprehension challenges
- Vocabulary challenges
- Complex text structure
- Multiple text features

Comprehension challenges. Comprehension is certainly affected by vocabulary, text structure, and text features. However, comprehension can also be dramatically affected by three additional factors: 1) the reader's background knowledge (or lack thereof); 2) the density of the text (e.g., if paragraphs are packed with complicated ideas with little explanation or if the text is very abstract); and, 3) the reader's ability to read strategically.

> Readers may not be in the habit of questioning the text, rereading, adjusting speed, identifying key words, using word-solving strategies, or annotating as they read — all strategies that good readers use to make sense of complex text.

If you've ever read an article or a book and come across a paragraph, section, or chapter that just didn't make sense to you, you've experienced this. This happens frequently when a reader has little background knowledge about a topic. For example, a reader familiar with motorcycles can read and understand a more challenging text about motorcycles than can someone who knows little about them. Limited comprehension can also occur when the text is unusually dense or unfamiliar. Science textbooks, primary sources, and Shakespearean sonnets are classic examples of genres that are challenging for some readers.

Lastly, the skill of the reader is a factor. When readers have limited "strategic and active moves" needed to understand a text or parts of it, they often "slide words" in front of their eyes but do not comprehend what they read. These readers may not be in the habit of questioning the text, rereading, adjusting reading speed to purpose and challenge, identifying key words and using word-solving strategies, or annotating or diagramming as they read—all strategies that good readers use to make sense of complex text. As you think about the comprehension challenges involved with a specific piece of text, think about the background knowledge of your students, the relative density of the text, and reading skills your students may or may not already have.

The other three categories—**vocabulary, text structure, and text features**—deal with specific aspects of a text that may make it difficult for students to read and comprehend. As stated earlier, readers need to understand 75–90% of the words that convey the meaning of the text to be able to understand the text.

Here are some examples of how these factors can make a text challenging to read and understand: A biography of a sports figure is typically set up in chronological order. This is typically easy for the reader to understand. However, depending on the sport being discussed, (e.g., rugby, lacrosse, cricket, curling), a reader unfamiliar with these sports might struggle to understand the vocabulary, the rules of the sport, or the context of the events being described. Conversely, the vocabulary of a novel may be fairly straightforward but the events may be described in a stream-of-consciousness or non-linear way that makes it challenging to figure out the order of events (e.g., *Catch 22*; *House on Mango Street*). Finally, although graphic novels are compelling to look at, their unique text features make understanding the narrative extremely difficult for many readers.

Your job is to think about the potential comprehension challenges in the texts you choose to use in your own classes. Examine the text carefully in order to identify potential stumbling blocks for your students. To help you, here are some questions you can ask yourself about each area. This is not an exhaustive list; it's simply intended to provide you with a place to start your analysis.

Text Challenge	Questions You Can Ask
Comprehension	• Is the text fiction or non-fiction? • Are there areas that seem to be particularly dense or complex? • Is this a topic that your students already know a lot about? • Are there some students who will struggle with this text? • What reading skills do your students have/need to understand this text? Do they need to be able to make connections? To visualize? Summarize? Separate fact from opinion?
Vocabulary	• What are the important technical terms (e.g., *anemone, bifurcation, quadratic equation*)? • What are the important academic words (e.g., *process, system, analyze, data, research, proposition, concept*)?
Text Structure	• How is the text set up? Is there an introduction followed by sections with a main idea and examples? Are there stanzas? Are there explanations accompanied by diagrams? Are there sections of explanation? Are ideas compared and contrasted within the text? Are there places where the author makes an argument? Are there sections of the text that describe cause and effect? • Is there a single structure throughout the text or many sub-structures to the text? • Is the text chronological in nature? Does it have tangents? Are there flashbacks?
Text Features	• Is there information in photos or drawings that your students will need to understand? • What types of graphs, tables, diagrams, or maps are present? Will your students need support to read them? • Are there terms in bold that will help student understand the text? Distract them? • How are the features of this text different than others you have asked students to read? How might these features be confusing for some?

3. What strategies or tools are best suited to address the challenges this text presents?

Now that you have started thinking about the specific challenges that a text may present for your students, what should you do with this information? How can you use it to plan? How can you use this information when teaching? Here you have three good choices: 1. Use instructional practices to support your students to work around the challenges in the text; 2. Model and teach students strategies for dealing with the challenges in the text; 3. Differentiate literacy support when you have students who read at widely varying levels.

- **Use instructional practices that provide supports for your students around the challenges in the text.**

  The first way to support your students in their efforts to comprehend challenging content area text is to make use of instructional practices that help scaffold their learning. These are located in each section of this Toolkit. Your task will be to select the instructional strategy or strategies that match what you are trying to accomplish. For instance, if you determine that your students need to build background knowledge in order to comprehend the text, you would look at *Part 2: Laying the Foundation* section of the Toolkit. An **Anticipation/Reaction Guide** or an **Interactive Word**

Wall might help you here. If you determine that students will need particular assistance with vocabulary, a **Word Sort** might assist you, as may a **Small Group Vocabulary Preview**. Finally, **Think-Alouds** can help you provide your students with a model of how an expert (you) tackles a content rich text. We suggest that you think about your students as readers, writers and thinkers, the challenges of your text and your purpose in having students read the text. Then identify some of the *Thinkquiry* tools that will help students be more successful in making meaning from the text.

- **Model and teach students strategies for dealing with these challenges.**

In addition to using instructional practices that provide direct support for your students, modeling and teaching them strategies they can use to meet these challenges independently is a critical component of building content knowledge. Vocabulary challenges might require students to keep a **Triple-Entry Vocabulary Journal** while **Analytic Graphic Organizers** may help provide clarity to certain types of characteristic text structures. Paired Reading is an excellent strategy students can use to work together to digest more complex texts.

> The first way to support your students in their efforts to comprehend challenging content area text is to make use of instructional practices that help scaffold their learning.

You can further differentiate literacy support when students use the same text by asking them to use different strategies as they read the text. Here the cognitive load of the text is mediated by what you ask students to do with the text. For example, a group of highly able readers may be asked to use an analytical strategy when reading while a group of less able readers may be asked to use a summarizing strategy. Or all students may be asked to take **Two-Column Notes** using different headings or to code the text but with different codes. Remember to utilize the five-stage *gradual release of responsibility* model when assigning the use of a strategy— and to provide clear modeling and guided practice where needed.

- **Differentiate literacy support—provide parallel texts for varying reading abilities.**

The reality is that you may have students with widely different reading abilities in the same class. One approach you can use is to provide parallel texts for students with varying reading abilities. This involves providing a variety of texts at different reading levels on the same topic for students to read and discuss. The advantage to doing this is that you are still asking all of your students to work with text, to think critically about the ideas being presented and to engage in high level discussion about content. By providing multiple texts, you remove the barrier that using a single complex text might present to struggling readers.

This approach might be a good one if your students vary widely in their literacy skills and you determine that the amount of scaffolding you would have to provide for your students outweighs the benefits of the content of the text itself. It makes it easier if you have some sort of reading assessment that informs you of students' reading levels. Even if you do not have this information, you can provide reading selections at different reading levels about the same topic as part of learning about the topic. For example, as part of a unit on epidemics, you might provide a complicated webpage on a specific disease outbreak, a chapter in the textbook about contagious diseases, and an article from a children's encyclopedia on contagion and hygiene. You could briefly describe each reading and the purpose for reading each source and either assign or have students choose which to read. Then, you have many options for organizing learning. For example, you can **Jigsaw** the reading assignments (see Part 4 of the Toolkit). First, students meet who completed the same reading and they determine the key points. Then students who read each of the sources meet in a group to share key points and summarize key ideas about contagious diseases before completing individual summaries or writing in response to a prompt. Other *Thinkquiry* collaborative routines, instructional practices, and student learning strategies that can also be productive when teaching the same content using multiple texts include **Save the Last Word for Me**, **Picture This!**, **Sum It Up**, **KWL Plus**, **Critical Thinking Cue Questions**, **Group Summarizing** and group completion of **Analytic Graphic Organizers** such as **Discussion Webs**, **Proposition Support Outlines**, **Concept Maps** and **Semantic Feature Analyses**.

If you decide to go this route, there are some excellent online resources that can help you find reading selections at different reading levels. One popular reading difficulty scale is the Lexile Framework from Metametrics (see www.lexile.com). The Lexile Framework is a scale for measuring both students' reading level and the relative difficulty of a text. The website contains a wealth of resources to assist educators in finding parallel materials. One of the more useful tools is the Lexile Analyzer, a tool that lets you paste in text (in rich text format only) from another source or to type in a text selection from a print resource and get a Lexile score for that text. Once you become familiar with the Lexile Framework and how it describes text difficulty, you will notice that an increasing number of publishers, article databases and educational websites include Lexile measures of their texts and will be able to use that information to select parallel texts for students to read and discuss as part of content learning.

Designing lesson plans that increase content learning

Planning—and implementing—engaging rigorous lessons that support both content learning and literacy development is not easy, especially when you are new to purposely integrating content literacy support into your instruction. First, you will want to identify the content standards you are addressing in the lesson or unit. Then you will want to think about the vocabulary demands inherent in the reading, writing, discussing, presenting, and/or researching that you want students to do as part of the unit of study. You will want to think about the types of text that students will need to read and understand as part of the unit—and the challenges that each text presents to readers. Or, conversely, you will need to think about the best use of text, given students' varying reading levels, that will support learning about the content. Then you will need to think about the instructional practices, student learning strategies, and collaborative routines you will use to get students to think deeply about the content using the texts you have selected.

You also want to think about what makes a good reading or writing assignment. Earlier in this section, we discussed the importance of engagement in the cycle of teaching and learning. For students to become effective content area readers, writers and thinkers, they need to complete assignments that build their literacy and learning skills while simultaneously supporting content learning (Irvin, Meltzer, Mickler, Phillips, & Dean, 2009). To do this, you need to design your assignments so that when completing the assignment, students

> By providing multiple texts, you remove the barrier that using a single complex text might present to struggling readers.

- Deepen and reinforce understanding of the content because the reading and writing is content focused;

- Improve their reading, writing, and critical thinking skills because they are using strategies and collaborative routines when completing the assignment; and,

- Engage with the content because the assignment design taps into the literacy and learning needs of adolescents.

Assignments with no obvious purpose are unlikely to motivate or engage students. Rigor is an important consideration as well. If an assignment is too easy or too hard, it does not inspire engagement. Generating assignments at the appropriate level of challenge is an art but one that is important to master if student engagement is the goal. Approaches to improved student engagement with content include

- Establishing an authentic reason to read or write.

- Reading or writing in conjunction with hands-on activities.

- Using collaborative learning routines to read and create text.

Student success with content area reading and writing assignments depends on the quality of the literacy instruction that supports students' learning. Reading and writing assignments should include (Irvin et al., 2009)

- Clear instructions, criteria, and examples of quality assignment responses to ensure students know what is expected, including a rubric for assessment.
- Content area reading or writing instruction within the context of completing the assignment (e.g., modeling of strategies, brainstorming of approaches, analysis of exemplars or rubrics).
- Coaching and feedback throughout that allows students to improve their comprehension and quality of work (e.g., use of the writing process, peer editing, paired reading, use of the assessment rubric prior to developing a final draft).

Finally, the importance of providing students with doable assignments cannot be overstated. Students, especially those who are not confident readers and writers, are more motivated to tackle assignments when they understand what they are expected to do and have the background knowledge and planning tools to be successful.

Thinking about how to best support student success when assigning content reading and writing takes practice. But the benefits to your students and their learning are well worth the effort. You may want to use the following template when planning your content instruction to help you ensure that you integrate appropriate content literacy support throughout your units of study.

Content Literacy Planning Template

Grade Level/Content Area/Unit Topic	
Learning Standards	

Content What specific content/concepts do you want students to understand and be able to apply as a result of instruction you will provide? Questions to Think About • When students ask why they need to know this content, what will you say? • How will students be exposed to and investigate this content? • What prior knowledge do students need? • What connections need to be made to other content within and across content areas and to real-life applications? • What vocabulary will be essential to understanding the target concepts? How will students learn this?	

Literacy Habits and Skills	

Literacy Outcomes How will students be expected to read, write, discuss, present, and engage in critical and creative thinking in relation to the content? Questions to Think About • What, specifically, will students be expected to read? To write? To discuss? To present? • Where will students be expected to engage in critical thinking (analysis, evaluation) and/or creative thinking (innovative application, synthesis)? • What modeling/explicit teaching will be necessary? • What literacy strategies do students know that they could apply to the tasks at hand? • How will you provide feedback and coaching along the way?	

Content Literacy Planning Template (continued)

Grade Level/Content Area/Unit Topic	
Meeting Adolescent Learning Needs	
Motivation and Engagement How will you include structured or supported choice, use of technology, collaborative learning, and authentic reasons to read and write as part of the learning of this content? Questions to Think About • What strategies do you plan to use or have students use related to motivation and engagement? • How do you plan to include differentiation (levels of reading, choices of topic, choices of which strategies or approaches to use to learn or demonstrate learning)?	
Assessment/Grading	
Quality Improvement How will you provide rubrics, exemplars, and clear expectations for the processes you expect students to use and the products that you expect students to produce?	
Resources	
Specific Texts and Materials/Technology/People Resources Needed to Support Success	
Notes Related to Facilitation of Instruction	

Evaluating your own classroom practice

It might be helpful to complete the following self-assessment of your own classroom practice to determine your current strengths and areas of challenge related to developing students' vocabulary development and reading comprehension skills within the context of content focused learning. That way you can reflect on where you have strengths that you can continue to build upon as well as where you might want to place additional emphasis.

After reading through the rubric and completing your ratings, we recommend that you select 2–3 areas where you want to change your practice. For those areas, look through the *Thinkquiry Toolkit* to identify some approaches you could use to increase your instructional support. List these and check periodically to make sure you are using the tools productively and frequently. At the end of the year, you can return to areas where you deliberately built your skills or changed your practice and think about how you would now rate yourself in these areas as well as evidence of how your instruction supported students to develop their literacy and learning skills.

Teacher Self Assessment Rubric

Directions

Please complete each individual component of the Teacher Self Assessment Rubric (CCSSO) by selecting the levels of frequency and proficiency that best describe your use of literacy best practices and instructional strategies to support student learning within your content area.

Frequency

1. I don't use this best practice.
2. I occasionally use this best practice.
3. I frequently use this best practice during a lesson or unit.
4. I consistently use this best practice during a lesson or unit.

Proficiency

1. I don't understand this literacy best practice or how to implement it in my classroom.
2. I am hesitant about implementing this best practice and would benefit from seeing this practice in action in my content area.
3. I am confident that the way I implement this best practice supports improved student learning in my classroom.
4. I am extremely confident when implementing this best practice and believe my use of this practice could serve as a model for others.

In the last column of the rubric, indicate the *Thinkquiry* tools you could use that support more frequent implementation of this practice.

Teacher Self Assessment Rubric

Literacy Component	Self-Assessment	*Thinkquiry* tools that support this practice
Vocabulary development		
Word rich environment I support students as they learn new vocabulary to better understand content concepts by using a variety of strategies to create a word-rich environment.	Frequency ① ② ③ ④ Proficiency ① ② ③ ④	
Explicit instruction I teach students how to use strategies to: • Connect new words to prior knowledge • Generate definitions from contextual cues and word analysis • Organize new words around core concepts	Frequency ① ② ③ ④ Proficiency ① ② ③ ④	
Repeated opportunities to interact with words I provide students with multiple opportunities to connect with, use, and remember content vocabulary.	Frequency ① ② ③ ④ Proficiency ① ② ③ ④	

Frequency

1. I don't use this best practice.
2. I occasionally use this best practice.
3. I frequently use this best practice during a lesson or unit.
4. I consistently use this best practice during a lesson or unit.

Proficiency

1. I don't understand this literacy best practice or how to implement it.
2. I am hesitant to implement this and would benefit from seeing it in action.
3. I am confident the way I implement this supports student learning.
4. I am extremely confident when implementing this and believe my use could serve as a model for others.

Teacher Self Assessment Rubric

Literacy Component	Self-Assessment	*Thinkquiry* tools that support this practice
Reading comprehension		
Use of high impact *before* reading strategies I teach and provide opportunities for students to use the following specific strategies to support their readiness for reading tasks: • Activating prior knowledge • Setting purpose for reading	Frequency ① ② ③ ④ Proficiency ① ② ③ ④	
Use of high impact *during* reading strategies I teach and provide opportunities for students to use the following specific strategies to improve comprehension during reading: • Identifying main ideas and supporting details/evidence by annotating/marking the text • Analyzing information by identifying fact, opinion, point of view, bias, generalizations • Asking questions to interact with text • Making inferences and drawing conclusions • Visualizing events, actions, relationships and/or patterns	Frequency ① ② ③ ④ Proficiency ① ② ③ ④	
Use of high impact *after* reading strategies I teach and provide opportunities for students to use the following specific strategies to help them respond to text after reading: • Reflecting about information and ideas in text • Using writing frequently in conjunction with reading • Summarizing information and concepts • Synthesizing ideas and information to enable transfer of concepts to new applications and situations	Frequency ① ② ③ ④ Proficiency ① ② ③ ④	

Frequency

1. I don't use this best practice.
2. I occasionally use this best practice.
3. I frequently use this best practice during a lesson or unit.
4. I consistently use this best practice during a lesson or unit.

Proficiency

1. I don't understand this literacy best practice or how to implement it.
2. I am hesitant to implement this and would benefit from seeing it in action.
3. I am confident the way I implement this supports student learning.
4. I am extremely confident when implementing this and believe my use could serve as a model for others.

Teacher Self Assessment Rubric

Literacy Component	Self-Assessment	*Thinkquiry* tools that support this practice
Reading comprehension		
Student-centered discussion I provide opportunities for students to discuss and share their understanding of content area texts through the use of strategies that encourage collaborative analysis, inquiry, and deep discussion.	Frequency ① ② ③ ④ Proficiency ① ② ③ ④	
Wide reading I expect students to engage in reading a variety of types of content area texts, including electronic text/media, and I provide in-class opportunities and resources for them to read.	Frequency ① ② ③ ④ Proficiency ① ② ③ ④	
Text structure and organization I preview the organization and patterns of text structure with students in order to support understanding of content and I do this whenever I assign a new type of text (e.g., article, short story, textbook, word problem, graph, chart, or electronic text/media).	Frequency ① ② ③ ④ Proficiency ① ② ③ ④	
Gradual release of responsibility I help students transfer reading comprehension skills and strategies for independent use through a process of gradual release. The gradual release model includes these steps. • Explicit teacher instruction and modeling • Guided small group practice • Individual student practice with feedback • Independent application by each student	Frequency ① ② ③ ④ Proficiency ① ② ③ ④	

Frequency

1. I don't use this best practice.
2. I occasionally use this best practice.
3. I frequently use this best practice during a lesson or unit.
4. I consistently use this best practice during a lesson or unit.

Proficiency

1. I don't understand this literacy best practice or how to implement it.
2. I am hesitant to implement this and would benefit from seeing it in action.
3. I am confident the way I implement this supports student learning.
4. I am extremely confident when implementing this and believe my use could serve as a model for others.

Part 2: Laying the Foundation

Part 2: Laying the Foundation

Introduction

Activating prior knowledge and building background knowledge prepares and motivates students to read and learn. You can prepare students to read and learn by

- Helping them identify what they already know
- Connecting what they will be studying to what they have studied previously
- Checking in on their current understanding of the topic at hand

Then you can target your instruction to remedy misconceptions, build on existing knowledge, and avoid repeating information that students already know.

In Part 1 of the Toolkit, you will find a selection of student learning strategies and teacher instructional practices as well as a collaborative routine, all of which will help students interact with vocabulary and text before reading and learning. Many of these tools can also be used throughout the reading and learning process to support understanding.

Helping students to reflect throughout reading and learning builds metacognition. Metacognition allows students to develop an awareness of self as a learner in relation to a given task and to think about the strategies one is using to accomplish the task. Developing metacognition strengthens learning skills and builds confidence. You can use the *Thinkquiry* tools in this section to guide students to reflect about their thinking. The tools prompt students to ask—and answer—questions, such as: What do I know? What do I need to know? What do I need to do? How can I do this? How well did it work? What did I learn? What can I do better next time?

In this section of the Toolkit, you will find the following approaches to supporting reading and learning:

	Reading & Learning Phases		
	Before	**During**	**After**
Student Learning Strategies			
Knowledge Rating Guide	✓	✓	✓
Frayer Model	✓		✓
Triple-Entry Vocabulary Journal	✓	✓	✓
Word Sort	✓		✓
Word Analysis	✓	✓	
Concept Map	✓	✓	✓
KWL Plus	✓	✓	✓
Quick Write	✓	✓	✓
Collaborative Routines			
Partner/Small Group Vocabulary Preview	✓		
Teacher Practices			
Think-Alouds	✓	✓	
Interactive Word Wall	✓	✓	✓
Chapter Preview/Tour	✓		
Anticipation/Reaction Guide	✓	✓	✓
Classroom Scenario			
Use of *Triple-Entry Vocabulary Journal* in a High School Science Classroom	✓	✓	✓

Knowledge Rating Guide

Description

A *before-*, *during-*, and *after-*reading activity in which students analyze their understanding of vocabulary words or concepts from the text or unit of study (Blachowicz, 1986).

Purpose

Use *before* reading to

- Introduce a list of key terms to students
- Determine students' knowledge of a word or concept
- Activate existing background knowledge
- Help students make connections to new concepts
- Assess learning when used *before* and *after* reading

Directions

1. Select a list of important terms from the text. Prepare a handout that lists the terms followed by three columns: *Know it/Use it*, *Can describe it/Don't use it*, *Don't know it/Don't use it*.

Term	Know it/ Use it	Can describe it/ Don't use it	Don't know it/ Don't use it

2. Give the **Knowledge Rating Guide** with the terms to students. Ask each student to rate their level of knowledge about each term by placing an X in the appropriate column.
3. Place students in small groups to talk about the terms and/or lead the class in a discussion about the terms that students know.
4. Ask students to read the text.
5. After reading the text, have students reexamine their sheets and see what words they can now define/use.

Extensions

- Ask students to write down definitions/explanations of terms they marked in the *Know it/Use it* column.
- Before discussing the terms as a class, have members of each small group discuss the terms and explain them to one another, and only discuss as a class the terms that no one knows.

Knowledge Rating Guide Template

Name _____   Date _____

Term	Know it/ Use it	Can describe it/ Don't use it	Don't know it/ Don't use it

Knowledge Rating Guide Content Examples

Mathematics

Elementary School

During a unit on geometry exploration, have students use a **Knowledge Rating Guide** description to help students monitor their understanding of key vocabulary words.

Term	Know it/Use it 👍	Can describe it ✋	Don't know it 👎
Congruent		✓	
Polygon		✓	
Attributes			✓

Middle School

Before a unit on ratio, proportion, and percents, give students a **Knowledge Rating Guide** description sheet with key mathematical terms they need to know at the end of the unit. Have them fill out the chart to assess their current understanding. For every term they do know, have them record their own definition in their math journal. Re-administer the guide later in the unit to assess growth with respect to vocabulary.

Term	Know it/Use it	Can describe it/Don't use it	Don't know it/Don't use it
Ratio			
Percent			
Fraction			

High School

Before studying a unit on number theory in a freshman integrated math class, provide the students with a **Knowledge Rating Guide** template with terms for a quick assessment of their understanding. For each of the terms students do not know, have them keep a **Triple-Entry Vocabulary Journal** as a personal vocabulary list. Assess students on their understanding of their personal terms throughout the unit.

Term	Know it/Use it	Can describe it/Don't use it	Don't know it/Don't use it
Real numbers			
Natural numbers			
Integers			
Rational numbers			
Irrational numbers			
Prime numbers			
Repeating numbers			

Knowledge Rating Guide Content Examples

Science

The science examples here were purposefully created for the same topic across the three grade spans for one strand in physics, "motion."

Elementary School: Motion

Before a series of lessons on motion, distribute the following **Knowledge Rating Guide**.

Term	Know it/Use it	Can describe it	Don't know it
Push			
Pull			
Force			
Direction			

Middle School: Motion

Use a similar template at the middle school level before starting a unit on motion.

Term	Know it/Use it	Can describe it/Don't use it	Don't know it/Don't use it
Force			
Friction			
Inertia			
Gravitational force			

High School: Motion

Challenge students to understand "motion" by studying the physics of driving a car. Incorporate concepts such as the distance traveled during braking at different speeds, the time required to stop at a changing traffic light, centripetal force on banked curves, and the science of skidding. Engage students at the beginning of the unit by including both core physics terms, as well as a few terms related to the context of the unit.

Term	Know it/Use it	Can describe it/Don't use it	Don't know it/Don't use it
Speed			
Acceleration			
Stopping distance			
Velocity			
Centripetal force			
Front-wheel drive			

Social Studies

Elementary School

Use to develop an understanding of students' prior knowledge when studying the geography of the United States.

Term	Know where it is 👍	Have heard of it 🖐	Never heard of it 👎
Mississippi River			
Rocky Mountains			
Everglades			

Middle School

Use to build an understanding of specific terms related to the study of ancient Mesopotamia.

Term	Know it well	Sort of know it	Don't know it
Cuneiform			
Stylus			
Ziggurat			

High School

Use as a review strategy to identify students' level of familiarity with specific technical terms before taking an exam on United States constitutional law.

Term	Can define it	Have heard of it	Never heard of it
Habeas corpus			
Article			
Amendment			
Ratify			

English Language Arts

Elementary School

Use to access students prior knowledge of basic literary terms.

Term	Know It/Use It 👍	Can Describe It ✋	Don't know it 👎
Point of View			
Conflict			
Plot			

Middle School

Use to help students assess their own understanding of critical academic skills.

Term	Know It/Use It	Can Describe It	Don't know it
Infer			
Analyze			
Synthesize			

High School

Use to access prior understanding of terms used in the study of Shakespeare.

Term	Know It/Use It	Can Describe It	Don't know it
Couplet			
Blank Verse			
Sonnet			

Frayer Model

S

Description

A **Frayer Model** is a graphic organizer that helps students form concepts and learn new vocabulary by using four quadrants on a chart to define examples, non-examples, characteristics, and non-characteristics of a word or concept. (Frayer, 1969)

Purpose

Use *before* or *after* reading to

- Help students form an understanding of an unknown word or concept
- Help students differentiate between a definition of a concept or vocabulary word and those characteristics that are associated with it

Directions

1. Select the word or concept to be defined using the **Frayer Model**.
2. Show the **Frayer Model** and explain the four quadrants.
3. Model how to use the **Frayer Model** to define a concept, using a simple example that students can understand.
4. Have students brainstorm a list of words and ideas related to the concept and then work together to complete a **Frayer Model**. Students may need to use a dictionary or glossary for clues.
5. Have students create a definition of the concept in their own words.

Extensions

- Describe the rationale for examples and non-examples.
- Use the **Frayer Model** as a note taking strategy during reading.
- Change the titles of the boxes to include concept development categories, such as etymology.

Frayer Model Example

Example of a **Frayer Model** graphic organizer.

Essential characteristics	Non-essential characteristics
• months • days of the week • dates placed on correct day of week for the year of the calendar	• photos or illustrations • dates of holidays • small box with former or next month • space to record notes or plans
Calendar	
Examples	Non-examples
• wall calendar • desk calendar • checkbook calendar	• yearbook • birthday chart • diary

Frayer Model

Frayer Model Template

Name _____   Date _____

Directions

Place the concept to be defined in the center square of the chart. Brainstorm a list of all the words you know that relate to the word or concept. Classify all of the brainstormed words into one of the four boxes in the chart. Use the information to write a definition of the concept.

Brainstorming List

Essential characteristics	Non-essential characteristics
Examples	Non-examples

Definition

Frayer Model Content Example

English Language Arts	Mathematics
During and *after* reading a novel independently after the class studies of literary devices Have students identify the predominant literary device used in their novel, such as figurative language, symbols, or personification. On poster board, they should write the device in the center of a **Frayer Model** template and complete the four quadrants, leading to a definition of the literary device. Post the charts around the classroom to remind students of the literary devices that can be used when writing.	*Before, during,* and *after* reading the relatively easy first chapter on coordinates and directed line segments in the complex textbook for analytic geometry Initiate a class habit of creating **Frayer Model** examples of analytic geometry terms that can be duplicated and kept in the front of their math notebook, starting with the easier terms that were taught in earlier math courses. Have students work in small groups to create definitions of the key terms, such as real numbers, rational numbers, periodic decimals, line segments, and coordinates. Gradually have students become independent in creating **Frayer Model** definitions of essential course concepts.
Science	**Social Studies**
Before and *after* a high school physics lesson sequence that teaches students about the concept of "acceleration." Early in the class, tell students they will be creating a **Frayer Model** for a term that has both a common as well as a very specific scientific meaning. Work with students to create a **Frayer Model** for the term, "acceleration." Toward the end of the lesson sequence, have students work in pairs to revisit their original **Frayer Model** for the term "acceleration," and highlight any ideas that have changed. Then have them create a new **Frayer Model** that demonstrates their new understanding of the scientific meaning of the term.	*Before, during,* and *after* reading about and taking a self-assessment of personality styles in a psychology course. Have each student create a **Frayer Model** about his/her personality style that was revealed in the self-assessment, working alone or with others of the same style, as they prefer. Then, group students with different styles together to share their **Frayer Models** and explain their differing traits and behaviors.

Triple-Entry Vocabulary Journal

Description

The **Triple-Entry Vocabulary Journal** is a strategy for learning new vocabulary that uses a three-column note taking format with columns for a word in context, definition in one's own words, and a picture, memory aid, or phrase related to the word.

Purpose

Use *before*, *during*, and *after* reading to

- Help students understand key words when reading text that may limit comprehension if they are not known
- Provide a more interactive way to learn new vocabulary than assign, define, and test
- Provide a way for students to cognitively process new words, resulting in more retention
- Help students develop a customized glossary to the text that provides words in context, applicable definitions, and personalized memory/study aids

Directions

1. Determine the key words students should understand while reading a selection.
2. Have students divide a notebook page into three columns. Label the columns
   - Word in context
   - Definition in my own words
   - Picture, memory aid, or phrase
3. Model the strategy with several words.
   - In the first column, write down the sentence(s) within which the word is found, and underline or circle the word. Note the page on which you found the word.
   - Look up the word in the dictionary. Choose the meaning that fits the context of the word in your text. Write down a definition of the word in your own words in the second column.
   - In the third column, draw an image, jot a phrase, or create a memory device that will help you remember the word and its meaning.
   - Have students practice the strategy, sharing their definitions and memory aids.

Extensions

- Have students select words they don't know while reading. Assign a predetermined number of total words and/or how many words per page/section/ chapter the student should select to enter in their **Triple-Entry Vocabulary Journal** for each reading selection.
- Jigsaw the word list to be found in a particular section of text and distribute different words to different students in small groups. Students then look through the text for the words before reading the selection to find the words, write them in the context of the sentence, and complete the strategy. Then the students in each group discuss and teach each other the words they will need to know for the text they are going to read.
- Have students compare and contrast each others' responses and discuss the words they found and did not know, supporting the development of word knowledge.

Triple-Entry Vocabulary Journal Template

Name _____   Date _____

Word in Context	Definition in My Words	Picture, Memory Aid, Phrase

Triple-Entry Vocabulary Journal Content Examples

Mathematics

Elementary School
During a unit on the number system, use **Triple-Entry Vocabulary Journal** entries to show how to use place values to read numbers.

Word in Context	Your Definition	Your Memory Aid
The **ones period** includes ones, tens, and hundreds.	A set of small numbers starting with 1 that goes up to 999	**1, 10, 100,** 9,999
The **thousands period** includes one thousands, ten thousands, and hundred thousands.	A set of bigger numbers starting from 1,000 to up a million	1,000, **10**,000, **100**,000, 999,999
The **millions period** includes one millions, ten millions, and hundred millions.	A set of really big numbers starting from 1 million up to a 1,000 million.	**1**,000,000, **10**,000,000 **100**,000,000, 999,999,999

Middle School
When reviewing fractions and equivalents, use **Triple-Entry Vocabulary Journal** entries to help students remember the meanings of the related math terms.

Word in Context	Your Definition	Your Memory Aid
A **fraction** is the name of a part of a whole or part of a set.	A part of something whose size is shown by a number	Pizza cut into slices
The **denominator** of the fraction shows the number of parts of the whole set.	The bottom number in a fraction that shows how many total parts there are	All 8 slices in a pizza pie
The **numerator** of the fraction shows the number of parts under consideration.	The top number in a fraction that shows the portion	2/8 means 2 slices of a pizza that is cut into 8 slices

High School
Use **Triple-Entry Vocabulary Journal** entries to record terminology when studying interest during a financial management unit.

Word in Context	Your Definition	Your Memory Aid
Simple interest is equal to the principal (amount loaned) times the rate (percent of interest charged) times time (number of years the money is loaned). I=PRT	When money is borrowed, a person must pay back the amount borrowed, plus an additional percentage.	If I borrow $20,000 to buy a car at 5% for 5 years, the total for the car is $20,000 plus $1,000 (.05 x 20,000) each year = $25,000 total.
Compound interest is interest paid on the principal plus the interest added to date. It can be compounded annually, semi-annually, quarterly, monthly, or daily.	When money is saved, a person gets an extra amount of money called interest that compounds, or grows bigger over time, as new interest is paid on the principal and all the previous interest.	Saving $1,000 at 5% interest for 25 years at simple interest, I get $50/year or $2,250 total. With compound interest, I get interest on the interest = $3,386.35 in 25 years.

Science

Elementary School

Before a science lab about light, have small groups work together to define key terms.

Word in Context	Your Definition	Your Memory Aid
Shine a flashlight on a clear glass, which is **transparent**. It lets light go through it so you see what's on the other side.	Transparent means you can see through it clearly.	A view from a window on a sunny day
Fill a glass with water and some watercolor paint. Can you see through the water? Yes, but not as well because the colored water is **translucent**. Only some light passes through.	Translucent means you can see through it a little, enough to see shapes but no detail.	The view from a window on a foggy day
Put only paint in the third glass. Paint is **opaque** and absorbs, or soaks up, most of the light and reflects the rest.	Opaque means you can't see through it.	The view from a window on a dark night

Middle School

During a study of ecosystems, using a text selection from *Sciencesaurus* to introduce the concept, have students download pictures that represent the parts of an ecosystem in their **Triple-Entry Vocabulary Journal.**

Word in Context	Your Definition	Your Memory Aid
A **species** is a group of organisms that can mate and produce offspring that, in turn, can produce more offspring.	Species are populations like humans or animals that have babies.	
All of the organisms of the same species that live in the same place at the same time make up a **population**.	A population is the whole group of the same type of species, like all the deer in a forest.	
Populations do not live alone. They share the environment with other populations to form a **community**.	A community is a group of several populations, like all the animals in a zoo.	

High School

Tell students they are to keep a daily technical vocabulary log called a **Triple-Entry Vocabulary Journal.** Let them work together during the first week as they study engineering careers, then expect them to continue on their own.

Word in Context	Your Definition	Your Memory Aid
Technologists work with existing technology to produce goods for society, like machines and equipment.	Technologists produce goods using technology that already exists.	Installation of office equipment in a new company to meet its needs
Engineers also apply technology for the betterment of society, but the engineer creates new technology through research, design, and development.	Engineers research and develop new technology, and inventions.	• Typewriter to computer • Film to digital camera • Maps to GPS systems

Social Studies

Elementary School

While engaging reluctant readers in a nonfiction chapter book about Harriet Tubman, have students create a **Triple-Entry Vocabulary Journal** and find pictures that fit each vocabulary word.

Word in Context	Your Definition	Your Memory Aid
Harriet's masters made her do housekeeping **chores**, but no one showed her what to do.	Work that has to be done around a house, like sweeping or washing dishes.	
They traveled by night and hid during the day, sometimes under the noses of people trying to catch them. Harriet used **disguises** and other tricks.	A costume or something that makes someone look different than they usually do.	

Middle School

When reading the Preamble to the Constitution, keep a **Triple-Entry Vocabulary Journal** of the key concepts.

Word in Context	Your Definition	Your Memory Aid
After the Shay's Rebellion uprising, the writers of the Constitution realized the national government must have the power to ensure **domestic tranquility**.	Peace and calm in the United States	 **A tranquil sea** The National Guard protects property, such as after hurricanes.
In order to form a **more perfect union,** the restatement of the concept of *E pluribus unum* (out of many, one), which many felt was important to get states to work together.	Establishing a national government with federal powers could stop independent states from quarreling, thus creating a more perfect union.	A C B becomes ABC

High School

In a high school economics class, help students understand entrepreneurship by keeping a **Triple-Entry Vocabulary Journal** of technical vocabulary.

Word in Context	Your Definition	Your Memory Aid
Dry cleaners, appliance repair shops, and other small firms that provide very modest returns to their owners are called **marginal firms**.	A marginal firm has a limited ability to produce significant profits past compensation for time.	
Attractive small firms offer substantial rewards to owner, earning $100,000 to $300,000 or more annually.	A small company that earns $100–300K after its costs is called an attractive small firm.	$100,000 to $300,000 profit
A few businesses have such potential for growth they are called **high-potential ventures** or **gazelles.**	Companies that grow at blinding speed, which make their founders rich when they go public.	 Facebook and YouTube

English Language Arts

Elementary School

During reading of Sewell's *Black Beauty*, help students learn new vocabulary using context clues.

Word in Context	Your Definition	Your Memory Aid
I love horses and it **riles** me to see them badly used.	Upsets and angers	Big ocean waves during a hurricane
Cruelty was the devil's own **trademark** and if we saw any one who took pleasure in cruelty we might know who he belonged to, for the devil was a murderer from the beginning...	A mark or picture that shows what someone is like	
Well, angry as I was, I was almost frightened. He roared and **bellowed** in such a style.	Make a loud scary noise	**MOOO!**

Middle School

To help students use key vocabulary terms from their reading when writing summaries of short stories, (e.g., London's *To Build a Fire*).

Word in Context	Your Definition	Your Memory Aid
His flesh was burning....The sensation developed into pain that grew **acute**.	Intense and strong	A skunk has an acute smell
He disrupted the **nucleus** of the little fire, the burning grasses and tiny twigs separating and scattering.	The center of something that holds it together	My mom is the nucleus of our family since Dad left

High School

When reading Hemingway's *The Old Man and the Sea*, use a **Triple-Entry Vocabulary Journal** to help students expand their descriptive vocabulary.

Word in Context	Your Definition	Your Memory Aid
The dark cloud of blood had settled and **dispersed** in the mile deep sea.	To break apart; dispel	A crowd running when a gunshot is heard
The old man's head was clear and good now and he was full of **resolution**, but he had little hope.	Determination that a future action will be done	New Year's Resolution

Word Sort

Description

Word Sort is a classification strategy where the teacher provides lists of words that students cluster together in meaningful ways to evolve main ideas or determine conceptual relationships (closed sort). The students may also sort the words by characteristics and meanings and then label the categories (open sort) (Gillet and Kita, 1979).

Purpose

Use *before* and *after* reading to

- Help students learn vocabulary by comparing, contrasting, and classifying words based on characteristics or meanings
- Help students recognize the relationships and differences between terms that are related to the same concept
- Develop students' ability to reason through analysis, classification, induction, and analogy
- Enhance students' interest in vocabulary development through a multi-sensory experience as they read, write, and manipulate words while sharing their thinking with others
- Develop divergent thinking when open sort is used

Directions

- Have students copy vocabulary terms onto index cards, one word per card.
- Have students sort the words into categories, either by providing the categories (closed sort) or having the students generate the categories (open sort).
- Have students share the reasoning and evidence for the way the vocabulary is sorted.
- Have students copy vocabulary words onto index cards or strips of paper, one for each word.

Example

Topic: Geometry—Solids, Circles, and Transformations		
Words to Sort		
pyramids	radius	translation
prism	diameter	lines of symmetry
reflection	surface area	isometric drawing
circumference	volume	cone
rotation	pi	rotational symmetry
Categories		
polyhedrons	circles/cylinders	transformations

Source: Weizer, 2003. Used with permission.

Extensions

- Have students sort the words into a Venn diagram, then summarize their findings in a **Quick Write**.
- Differentiation suggestion: Match the complexity of the vocabulary terms used in the sorts to students' varied instructional levels.

Word Sort Template

Name _____   Date _____

Categories

Words to Sort

Word Sort Content Examples

Mathematics

Open **Word Sort** (students determine the categories after discussing the words and sorting them into affiliate clusters)

Topic: Geometry and Measurement — Solid Figures and Processes of Measurement

Words to Sort		
prisms	base	lateral faces
platonic solids	cone	cylinder
sphere	pyramid	polygons
circumference	pi	surface area
volume	cubic unit	vertex

Science

Open Word Sort (students determine the categories after discussing the words and sorting them into affiliate clusters)

Topic: Erosion and Weathering

Words to Sort		
aquifer	glacier	esker
leaching	terracing	channel
abrasion	climate	oxidation
soil	striation	outwash

Social Studies

Closed **Word Sort** (teacher determines categories for students to sort under)

Topic: Early American History

Categories		
People	Places	Common concepts
Words to Sort		
Jamestown	Quakers	Pilgrims
colony	Puritans	indentured servitude
slaves	Plymouth	haven
epidemic	imports/exports	Pennsylvania

English Language Arts

Closed **Word Sort** (teacher determines categories for students to sort under)

Topic: *Anne Frank—The Diary of a Young Girl* by Anne Frank

Categories		
Mood	Illness	Personality trait
Words to Sort		
melancholy	poignant	diphtheria
despondent	hypochondria	superficial
pensive	dejected	jocular
malaria	fanatic	fatalistic

This example was developed by Roz Weizer. Used with permission.

Word Analysis

Description

The **Word Analysis** strategy is a way of analyzing the structure of unknown words to derive their meaning. Students deconstruct words into prefixes, roots, and suffixes and make connections between these and other words sharing similar parts. Readers often combine this strategy with the contextual analysis of the sentence or passage in which the word is found in a text.

Purpose

Use *before* or *during* reading to

- Define unknown words
- Make words memorable through understanding the parts that make up the word
- Connect new vocabulary to words already known
- Improve reading fluency
- Improve reading comprehension

Directions

1. Identify words in an upcoming reading selection that can be analyzed using their roots and affixes (prefix or suffix).

2. Focus instruction on identifying the root word and seeing how the prefix and suffix function together with the root to create the meaning of the word. Model this for the class.

3. Have students practice covering the prefixes and suffixes to see the root words, then follow with practice in adding and removing prefixes and suffixes and discussing how this changes the meaning of the word. Do this as a class and then have students continue in pairs or small groups, putting their best guess of the meaning in the appropriate column on the template. Then review the definitions and see how close the guesses were, making sure students correct and refine definitions as necessary.

4. Once students are comfortable with **Word Analysis**, teach them the specific root words that relate to the content area and topic(s) of learning by providing practice with many words with the same root and/or affix. Ask students to generate other words that use the same root or affix, divide the list into groups of words, and have pairs or small groups analyze how each group of words is similar or different. This process of comparing words not only helps students more than memorizing a definition would, but also contributes to an understanding of how word parts influence word meaning and reinforces words related to the same concept.

Extensions

- Combine the study of word parts with instruction in the use of context clues.
- Use vocabulary instruction strategies as appropriate to the specific words: **Word Analysis** for a compound word like *piecemeal* or *uncomfortable* and *discomfort*; a **Concept Definition Map** or **Frayer Model** for more complex concepts like *freedom* or *power*; and a **Triple-Entry Vocabulary Journal** or **Interactive Word Wall** for technical terms that pertain to a specific topic like *algebra* or *electricity*

Word Analysis Template

Name _____ Date _____

Content Unit/Topic _____

Directions

Write the unknown vocabulary words in the left column. Divide the word into its parts and then develop a possible definition for the word.

Word	Prefix	Root	Suffix	Definition

Word Analysis – Frequent Affixes and Roots

Prefixes		Suffixes	
a-, an-	mono-	-able, -ible	-ion, -tion, -ation, -ition
anti-	non-	-al, -ial	-ity, -ty
bi-	out-	-ed	-ive, -ative, -itive
co-	over-	-en	-less
counter-	pre-	-er, ier	-ly
de-	pro-	-er, -or	-ment
dis-	re-	-est	-ness
en-, em-	semi-	-ful	-ous, -eous, -ious
ex-	sub-	-ic	-s, -es
fore-	super-	-ing	-y
in-, im-	syn-		
in-, im-, il-, ir-	tele-		
inter-	trans-		
mid-	un-		
mis-	under-		

Common Greek and Latin Roots in English

Root	Meaning	Origin
aud	hear	Latin
astro, aster	star	Greek
auto	self	Latin
bene	good	Latin
bio	life	Greek
chrono	time	Greek
dict	speak, tell	Latin
duc	lead, make	Latin
gen	give birth	Latin
geo	earth	Greek
graph	write	Greek
jur, jus	law	Latin
luc	light	Latin
man	hand	Latin
meter	measure	Greek
min	little, small	Latin
mit, mis	send	Latin
omni	all	Latin
ped	foot	Latin
phon	sound	Greek
photo	light	Greek
port	carry	Latin
qui	quiet	Latin
scrib, script	write	Latin
sens	feel	Latin
spect	see	Latin
struct	build, form	Latin
tele	far off	Greek
terr	earth	Latin
vac	empty	Latin
vid, vis	see	Latin

Thinkquiry Toolkit 1

KWL Plus

Description

KWL is a reading/thinking strategy that provides a three or four -column graphic organizer for students to list 1) what they **know (K)** about a topic; 2) what they **want (W)** to learn about a topic; 3) what they **learned (L)** about a topic after instruction or reading. **KWL Plus** adds mapping and summarization to the original KWL strategy. This helps students restructure text and rewrite to process information (Carr & Ogle, 1987).

Purpose

Use *before*, *during*, and *after* reading to

- Activate and/or assess prior knowledge
- Provide preview of vocabulary or concepts
- Provide purpose for reading based on student knowledge/interest
- Help students be aware of their learning progress
- Check for misconceptions
- Support flexible grouping for differentiated instruction

Directions

1. After an initial discussion, short reading, or video to activate prior knowledge about the topic, distribute copies of a **KWL Plus** chart, formatted with four columns with the headings *What I Know, What I Want to Know, What I Learned, What I Still Wonder About.*

2. Tell students the topic you want them to think about and ask them to fill in the **K** column, listing what they already know about the topic.

3. Ask students to think about what they would like to learn about the topic. Encourage them to think of at least one idea to write in the **W** column. Have students brainstorm where to find this information and list this in the chart. Note: can change W to N—*What They Need to Know.*

4. Students read the selection(s) provided or assigned and fill in the **L** column of the chart, listing the things they learned from the reading.

5. Discuss the accuracy of students' prior knowledge. If they still have questions, ask them to add these to the **+** column, *What I Still Wonder About.*

6. Students then use the **KWL Plus** worksheet to construct a concept map that categorizes all the information they have learned about the topic.

Extensions

- Have students write a summary about the topic.
- Ask students to complete a **Quick Write** that describes the learning process: What did you already know before reading? What did you want to learn about? How did you approach learning about it? What did you find out?

KWL Plus Template

Name _____ Date _____

Directions

1. List what you **know (K)** about a topic, what you **want (W)** to learn about a topic, what you **learned (L)** about a topic after reading about it, and what you still wonder (**+**) about.

2. Create a **Concept Map** of your understanding of the topic.

K What I *Know*	W What I *Want* to Know	L What I *Learned*	+ What I Still Wonder About

Concept Map

KWL Plus Content Example

Mathematics

During an introduction to statistics, use **KWL Plus** to help students identify questions they'd like to answer about their class or school.

Topic: Pet Ownership

K	W	L	+
• Lots of people have pets • I have a dog and a cat • You can have more than one pet, only one, or none. • My friend, Carmen, has a cat.	• What percentage of students in our class have pets? • What is the most popular type of pet?	• 70% of students have pets. • There are more cats owned by our class members than any other animal, but more families have a dog.	• Do people with more than one pet have specific combinations of pets more frequently (like a dog and a cat)? • Are boys or girls in our class more likely to have a certain kind of pet?

Science

Use **KWL Plus** to build students' capacity to think about science in terms of proposing questions, answering them, and thinking of new questions.

Topic: Killer Whales

K	W	L	+
• Live in oceans • Are vicious • Eat other whales • Are mammals	• What kind of fish do they eat? • How long do they live? • How do they breathe?	• Weigh 10,000 lbs. And get 30 ft. Long • Squids, seals and dolphins • Are carnivorous • Breathe through blow holes • Have echolocation • Found in oceans • Are warm-blooded • Have good vision under water	• Why do they attack people? • How fast can they swim?

Social Studies

Before and during the study of the formation of the United States Constitution, have students fill out the first two columns of the **KWL Plus** chart. As students interact with texts and primary source documents, talk as a class about what these things tell them about the questions they originally asked. Afterwards, have students identify new questions they will explore individually. Use these questions as the basis for *poster sessions* on this aspect of American History.

Topic: United States Constitution

K	W	L	+
• It was written a long time ago. • It's why we have the kind of government we have.	• Who wrote the constitution? • How did they think of it? • Is Freedom of Speech in the Constitution? • A group of 55 men sort of wrote it together.	• They got lots of the ideas from John Locke, a philosopher, and they took some ideas from England's government. • Freedom of speech is in the Bill of Rights. That is a collection of amendments that got added soon after the Constitution was written.	• Was it hard to agree on all the different parts? • When people had different ideas, how did they decide what to do? • What are the other parts of the Bill of Rights?

English Language Arts

Before, during, and after reading a collection of works by Shel Silverstein, have students complete what they know and want to know about the author. During reading, have students read short biographical pieces and collect what they are learning in the **KWL Plus** template. As a class, identify the most pressing questions students still have and look for new texts or other resources to answer the questions.

Topic: Shel Silverstein

K	W	L	+
• Writes poetry • Draws pictures in his books • Is funny	• When did he start writing poems? • Why did he write and draw? • Does he still write?	• Started writing when he was twelve because he wasn't good at baseball • He died in 1999.	• How did he get his poems into books? • If you want to be a poet, what do you have to do?

Concept Map

Description

A visual web or map that shows the relationships between different aspects of a key concept to help learners understand the concept on a deeper level and to relate new information learned about the concept to older information already known.

Purpose

Use *before*, *during*, or *after reading* to

- Take notes in a structured way related to a key concept in order to understand its parts
- Better understand the relationships between and among the ideas that are presented in a single text or across multiple texts about the same concept
- Synthesize knowledge and information
- Generate ideas about a topic before writing
- Represent a complex concept in a visual format
- Demonstrate understanding of a concept (when used as an assessment)

Directions

1. Create a simple concept map to model the strategy to students.
2. Explain that the first step is to select a central topic, concept, or theme and list it in the center of the map.
3. Model how to define several main ideas related to the concept. Do so by adding them on multiple lines outward from the central circle.
4. Model how to then add specific details to the main ideas.
5. Give students a real-life concept they already understand and have them practice creating a **Concept Map**. Have them share their results with one another.
6. Refer students to a short text reading that explains a concept. Have students work in pairs or small groups to create a **Concept Map**.
7. Have students create a **Concept Map** for a longer passage of several paragraphs or a page.
8. Ask students to independently create a **Concept Map** based on their reading.

Extensions

- Have students compare and contrast their **Concept Maps** with others' **Concept Maps**.
- Use **Concept Maps** as an assessment of learning.
- Have students map two or three concepts and show how they relate to one another.
- Have students use **Concept Maps** for planning and organizing writing.
- Have students use mapping software, such as Inspiration, to create maps.
- Use **Concept Maps** to collaboratively brainstorm existing knowledge before reading and add to the map as students read.
- Brainstorm with students a rubric for assessing **Concept Maps**.

Concept Map Template

Name _____ Date _____

Directions

Put the concept word in the center. Decide what primary categories are related to the concept and list them on the branches. Add extra branches if you need them. Then, on the small branches add descriptive words or examples that further describe each category.

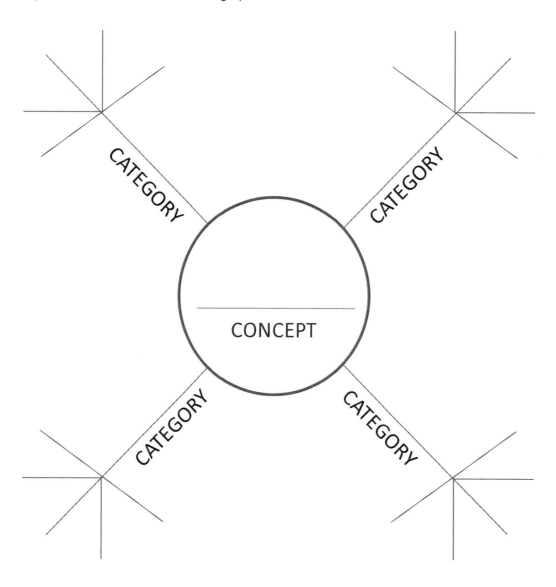

Concept Map Content Examples

Mathematics

Elementary School

Before and *during* a unit on Patterns

Have students work in groups to identify descriptive words and examples for each category. Have students put their map on chart paper and post in the room. As the unit progresses, have groups meet for a few minutes at the start or end of each lesson to add additional categories or descriptive words to the map.

Middle School

Before a unit on Comparing Quantities

Provide students with numerous examples of quantity comparisons. Have students work in groups to sort the examples into categories and complete the **Concept Map**. As a large group, discuss the category names students came up with and connect them to the terms they will be learning in the unit.

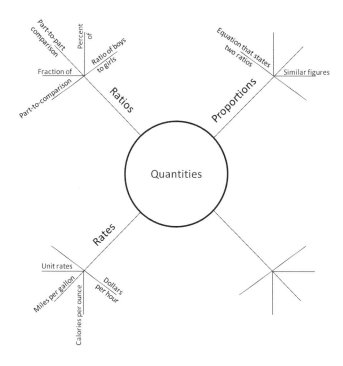

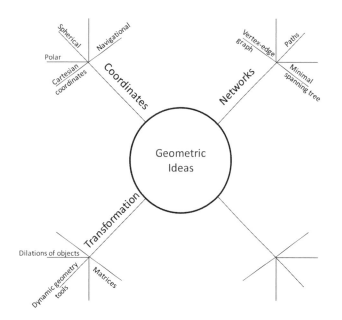

High School

During a section about how to represent Geometric Ideas

Provide students with a blank **Concept Map** template with the concept *Representing Geometric Ideas*. Next to the concept, make a list of words related to the concept. Have students work in small groups to determine which are categories and which are descriptive words and put them in the appropriate places on the **Concept Map**.

Social Studies

Elementary School

Central concept: Newspapers

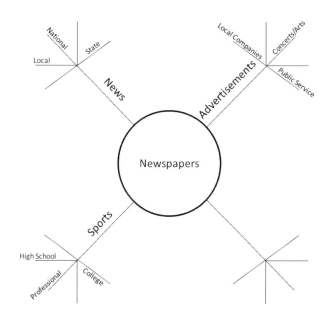

Middle School

Central concept: Gods of Greek Mythology

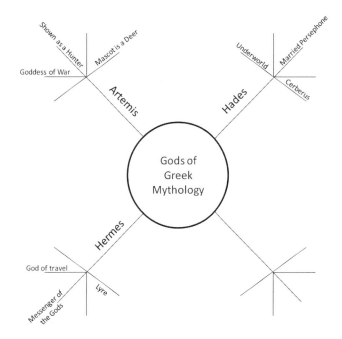

High School

Central concept: Inequity

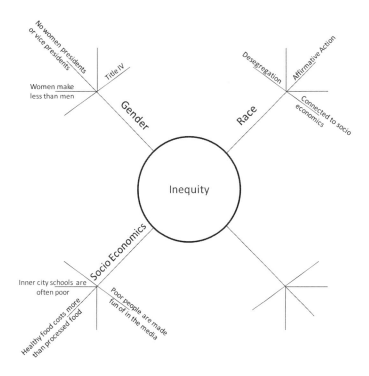

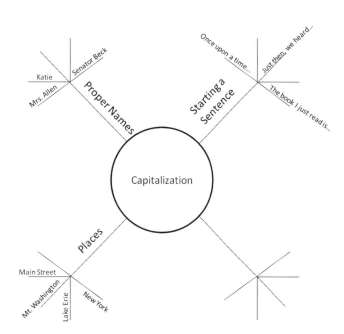

English Language Arts

Elementary School

During a unit on writing mechanics, create **Concept Maps** together as a class after studying different aspects of punctuation to solidify the main ideas.

Middle School

Use to clarify characters in a novel (e.g., *Holes* Sachar, L. (1998). *Holes*. New York: Random House).

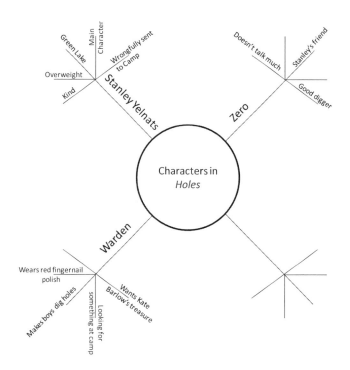

High School

After a unit where several pieces are read, ask students to work in small groups to represent Types of Conflict.

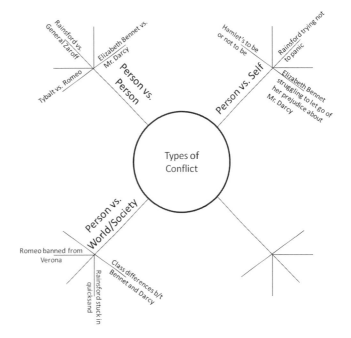

Science

Use **Concept Maps** in science before reading and learning to help students make their thinking explicit and as a record so that after reading and learning they can reflect about how their thinking has changed.

Elementary School: Water Cycle

Before studying about the water cycle, provide each student with a copy of the Concept Map Template and a set of cards with key terms: water, liquid, gas, air, vapor, heat, cool, disappear. Have students arrange their cards on to show relationships between the terms, and then ask them to record the arrangement onto the template. Later in the unit, following hands-on experiences and discussions, have students read an article that summarizes the water cycle. Ask students to use the cards again with a clean template to demonstrate how their thinking has changed.

Middle School: Seasons

Before studying about seasons, have students brainstorm a list of ideas related to the causes of seasons on a piece of paper and then create a Concept Map of their own, showing relationships between those concepts. After learning about phenomena such as Earth's shape, Earth's rotation (night and day), sun-earth distance, shape of earth's orbit, temperature and photoperiod variations, tilted earth, and angle of sunlight, have students repeat the process of creating a Concept Map for "seasons." Conclude by having students use their map to plan and organize a written summary about the causes of seasons, including an explanation of how their thinking shifted from where they started.

High School: Chemical Reactions

Begin a unit about chemical reactions by providing pairs of students with a template listing "Chemical Reactions" in the center, as well as a set of cards on which are written key terms such as: atom, molecule, nucleus, proton, neutron, electron, configuration, bond, energy level, interaction. Have students use cards that are familiar to show their initial understanding of the relationships between these ideas. Have them use the completed Concept Map template as an organizer to support them in writing a summary of their current understanding, including a reflection on their initial ideas and how their thinking may have changed.

Quick Write

S

Description

A versatile strategy used to develop writing fluency, to build the habit of reflection into a learning experience, and to informally assess student thinking. The strategy asks learners to respond in 2–10 minutes to an open-ended question or prompt posed by the teacher *before*, *during*, or *after* reading.

Purpose

Use *before*, *during*, and *after* reading to

- Activate prior knowledge by preparing students for reading, writing, or a discussion
- Help students make personal connections
- Promote reflection about key content concepts
- Encourage critical thinking
- Organize ideas for better comprehension
- Increase background knowledge when shared
- Synthesize learning and demonstrate understanding of key concepts
- Reinforce vocabulary
- Provide a purpose for reading
- Assess student knowledge on the topic prior to reading

Directions

1. Explain that a **Quick Write** engages students in thinking about a content topic before, during, and after reading. Stress that in a **Quick Write**, students respond to a question or prompt related to the text by writing down whatever comes to their minds without organizing it too much or worrying about grammar. Typically, a **Quick Write** is graded only for completion, not for quality or accuracy
2. Select a topic related to the text being studied and define the purpose for the **Quick Write**.
   Examples
   - Summarize what was learned
   - Connect to background information or students' lives
   - Explain content concepts or vocabulary
   - Make predictions, inferences, and hypotheses
   - Pose a question that addresses a key point in the reading selection
3. Tell the students how long they will have to do the writing, typically 2–10 minutes.
4. Use the **Quick Write** as part of instruction, assessment, and discussion.

Extensions

- **Quick Writes** can be assigned as part of students' Learning Logs or Journals.
- **Quick Writes** can be used to think/brainstorm for a **Think-Pair-Share**.
- Students can generate their own **Quick Write** questions and prompts.
- Students can share their responses in small groups and compare their answers
- Students can work in small groups to create a **Quick Write**, with each student offering one sentence in a round-robin fashion.

Quick Write Content Examples

Mathematics

- How do you divide something into pieces?
- How much is a million?
- Describe the differences between a factor and a multiple?
- If you flip a coin 10 times, how many times do you think it will come up "heads?" Why do you think so?
- What's a prime number?
- What do you know about Pascal's Triangle?
- What does it mean to "square" something? For example, what does x2 mean?

Science

- *Before* studying an Earth science unit about weathering, erosion and deposition, have students do a Quick Write in their science notebook, responding to the following prompt: "Does the surface of the Earth change? How do you know? What evidence do you have?"
- *After* a lesson on erosion, have students do a **Quick Write** on how erosion changes the surface of the earth.
- *Before* a study about the cross-discipline theme of "systems," elicit student thinking and prior knowledge by having them respond to a **Quick Write**: "Where have you heard the word system before? How would you explain what it means?"
- *Before* studying a science-in-society unit, elicit students' prior knowledge using the following **Quick Write** prompt: There are many conversations going on right now about global climate change and how to deal with it. "What do you think global climate change is? How is the global climate changing? How do you know?"

Social Studies

- We are going to study recent efforts to achieve a Middle East Peace Accord. Who are the key political figures you think are likely to influence this effort?
- Imagine that you lived 30,000 years ago during the Stone Age. How did you use natural resources to survive?

English Language Arts

- Characters in literature make decisions that have consequences for themselves and others. What is a decision you made that had unanticipated consequences, both for yourself and others?
- Describe a time you had to piece together clues to solve a mystery in your own life.

Partner/Small Group Vocabulary Preview

Description

The **Partner/Small Group Vocabulary Preview** is a *before* reading strategy where students collaboratively discuss and define vocabulary before reading a selection, so that text comprehension during reading is enhanced.

Purpose

Use *before* reading to

- Build word knowledge prior to reading
- Provide opportunities for collaborative analysis of new vocabulary, using contextual and structural clues in the text as well as prior knowledge
- Help struggling readers learn how to define words from the text context
- Provide an interactive way to preview content reading selections and stimulate interest in reading

Directions

1. Create a list of vocabulary words that students will need to understand in order to comprehend the text.
2. Use a **Think-Aloud** to model what you want students to do. Analyze 4–5 words using structural analysis (prefixes, affixes, roots) and context clues.
3. Have students work with partners or small groups to locate the vocabulary words. As each one is found, the group analyzes the context in which the word is used.
4. Students discuss whether anyone in the group can define the vocabulary term in his/her own words. All students who know the word should share their ideas and agree on a common definition. Students take notes on the definitions.
5. If no one in the group can define a word, students access other classroom resources that might help them understand it, such as a dictionary or text glossary. The definition should then be stated in their own words.
6. Bring the students together for a whole class discussion of the vocabulary terms and discuss the various definitions. Students should check the definitions they wrote in their notes to be sure they are accurate and add new information from the class discussion.

Extensions

- Have students do a **Quick Write** to summarize the concept that connects the vocabulary words together.
- Have students record their definitions in a **Triple-Entry Vocabulary Journal** that includes an example or illustration of the application of the words to help recall.
- Develop a **Word Wall** with the vocabulary terms and students' definitions.
- Create a **Concept Definition Map** for the most difficult words.
- Have students compare their definitions with dictionary definitions.

Partner/Small Group Vocabulary Preview Template

Name _____ Date _____

Reading selection _____ Pages ___ – ___

Directions

Preview the reading selection to find new vocabulary terms and try to figure out what they mean. Analyze each word to see if there are structural clues, such as a prefix, suffix, or root. Then locate context clues in the sentence or nearby sentences. Discuss the word to find out what anyone already knows about its meaning. You may also use resources like the text glossary or a dictionary. Then define the terms in your own words on this chart.

Vocabulary term	Clues to its meaning
Definition in your own words	

Vocabulary term	Clues to its meaning
Definition in your own words	

Vocabulary term	Clues to its meaning
Definition in your own words	

Think-Aloud

Description

Think-Aloud is a modeling strategy designed to help students learn how to monitor comprehension, engage actively with text, and direct their thinking as they work through the process of understanding a text.

Purpose

Use *during* reading to

- Engage students actively in thinking about how they are constructing meaning from text
- Enhance metacognitive awareness as students consider what they know and don't know
- Help students learn specific strategies for reading comprehension
- Enhance content area learning and comprehension

Directions

1. Consider what students need to know about what to do during the reading task.
   - What meaning do you want them to construct from the content?
   - What reading comprehension strategy do you want them to learn and use?
2. Identify where you might pause during the passage to **Think Aloud** for your students.
   - Think about your own experiences related to the content/strategy.
   - Take what you know implicitly and make it explicit for students.
3. Mark the pauses with a sticky note with a short notation about what you'll say.
4. Explicitly explain the **Think-Aloud** strategy to the students before using it.
   - Tell students about the strategy, why it helps, and when to use it.
   - Explain that you'll show them what's going on inside your head as you use a strategy to construct meaning.
5. Read the text aloud to the students as you model the **Think-Aloud**.
   - Provide all students with a copy of the text to follow along *OR*
   - Project the text on a screen so all can visually follow along.
6. Model the chosen thinking tasks by stopping to articulate what's going on in your head.
7. Give guidelines for students to practice doing a silent **Think-Aloud**, using sticky notes to guide the strategy.
   - Write down thoughts, questions, and connections as you read
   - Have a "conversation" with the author. Write down what you would say to him/her
   - Note your reading "moves"—where do you skim, have questions about words, get confused

Extension

- Pair students to read a passage together and present **Think-Alouds** to each other, giving each other feedback based on a checklist or rubric.

Planning for Think-Aloud

Before the Think-Aloud

1. Plan for (a) or (b)

   a. How do you want students to read and think about the content?

   b. What reading comprehension or vocabulary strategy do you want students to learn and use?

2. Identify where you might pause as you read the passage to "think aloud" for your students. You might think aloud about your own experiences related to both the content and the strategy or take what you know implicitly and make it explicit for students. Record main points you want to make here or mark where you plan to pause with a sticky-note with a short notation of what you'll say.

During the Think-Aloud

3. Explicitly explain the Think-Aloud strategy before using it

   - Tell students what strategy you will model, why it helps, and when to use it
   - Explain that you'll show them what's going on inside your head to construct meaning

4. Read the text with the students as you do the **Think-Aloud**

   - Give students a copy of the text to follow along or put the text on an overhead projector so they can visually follow along
   - Model by stopping to articulate what's going on in your head related to 1a or 1b.

After the Think-Aloud

5. Ask students what you did that was most helpful for their learning of 1a) how to read and think about the content or 1b) how to use a specific strategy.

Think-Aloud Content Examples

Mathematics

Before asking students to determine the functions shown by various graphs

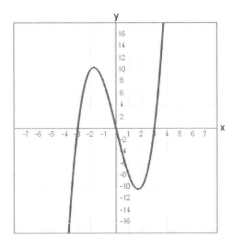

Let's take a look at this graph and try to figure out the function that is being represented. I notice this appears to be an "odd function" because it has rotational symmetry around the origin. So I know that only terms with odd exponents will appear. I am going to guess it is probably a cubic polynomial because it does not look like it zooms up the way it would with a higher exponent like x^5 or x^7 and there are only three points that it crosses the x axis. If it is x^3, I need to ask if y= x(x+3) (x-3) because the graph hits the points 3, 0 and -3, 0. What value do I get when I plug in 2 to this equation? It turns out that I get -10, which appears to be on the graph. If the point was actually -20, I would need something else in my equation, like -2. My hypothesis is that this graph represents the function fx=x^3 – 9x.

Science

Before asking students to read other informational websites about photosynthesis

I am going to click on the Thinkquest website (http://www.thinkquest.org) so you can see an introduction to Photosynthesis that was created by other students. I am going to do a **Think-Aloud** with the first paragraph so you can see how I want you to work with the text you find on the website I assigned you.

Animals *inhale oxygen* and *exhale carbon dioxide*. Well I know what inhale and exhale means and we have discussed respiration in animals. But I don't know what this has to do with plants. Green plants are the only plants that produce oxygen and make food, which is called *photosynthesis*. Aha! So plants make the oxygen animals breathe. Huh! And they do it through this process called photosynthesis. Photosynthesis means "'putting together with light.'" I think I will go back and click on the link to get a definition of photosynthesis. Okay I get it, sort of. And the diagram on the side helps gives me the sense of it. I hope the next part of the article gives more detail. I am going to scan ahead to see how complicated this gets. Whoa. Lots of vocabulary I do not know coming up. Chloroplasts, chlorophyll, stomata. I think I'll click on the links before reading and put these in my **Triple-Entry Vocabulary Journal**. Then I can refer to the meanings when I read the rest of the article.

Social Studies

Before asking students to code newspaper editorials related to the upcoming gubernatorial election

I am going to model for you how I want you to **Code** when you are reading these newspaper editorials. I would like you to use a check for something you agree with, an X for something you disagree with, an F for fact and an O for opinion. You may want to read the article twice so you can do the coding in two parts. Okay, as I read this first line (read the line), I am thinking that this person must be a conservative because of the insistence he is placing on the need to cut taxes. This is his opinion, so I will code this part with an O. And I think I agree, so I will put a check besides this. (Read the next two sentences.) Here he states that the candidate he favors will cut the car registration tax if he wins. But this is strange because I think that the car tax is levied by towns, not the state. So I will mark this with an X.

Working with a partner, please select and read one of the editorials and talk through how you will code the article. Use two different pen colors so I can see what you each were thinking throughout. Then we will do a compilation of the types of facts and opinions that were shared in the editorials in the past week and get a sense of what you find to be persuasive as you read.

English Language Arts

Before asking students to read haiku

So I know that a classic haiku has three lines. Line 1 has 5 syllables, line 2 has 7 syllables, and line 3 has 5 syllables. Only 17 syllables total. I know that haiku are often about nature or of a personal experience. I want to look more deeply at a few haiku before I try to write one myself. This one was a runner up in the Earth Day haiku competition: *Blue marble in space – spinning its face to the sun – irreplaceable.* I like how when I say the words out loud, *space* and *irreplaceable* have the same sound. And I like how the "s" sound is repeated – *space, spinning, face, sun, irreplaceable.* I like the sense of the earth as a "blue marble in space" – I can picture that. And marbles can be precious and valuable, which is how I think of our planet.

I found this one on a website and I really like it, too. It reminds me of my cat: *Old tomcat sitting – Watched the autumn leaves blow by – Wishing they were mice.* I can picture this so clearly! The cat, the leaves – and the wish! I like the way the last two lines both begin with "w" and the repetition of the two kinds of "i" sound – *sitting* and *wishing* as well as *by* and *mice.*

So haiku can present a sharp concise image or feeling. I was not sure if I could write something powerful in such a small number of words, but I think it is possible. I am going to choose my topic – winter – and then start brainstorming words and images. *White, ice, snow, quiet, footprints, skiing, warmth, hats, mittens, scarves, sledding, crunch.* Now I am going to think of some phrases*: iron gray billows of sky, haunting silence, cold crystals drip.* Next I am going to play with the words and phrases, keeping in mind the 5–7–5 syllable pattern, and then see what I will have.

I would like you to choose a partner and a topic and do the same thing with words and images you select. We will share our efforts before the end of class. If you want to look at some more haiku for inspiration, you are welcome to look at the books I have put on the table.

Interactive Word Wall

Description

A **Word Wall** is a systematically organized collection of displayed words. Both students and teachers can suggest additions to **Word Walls**. Students are asked to interact with words on the Word Wall on an ongoing basis. In this way, the words become an integral part of students' reading, writing, and speaking vocabulary.

Purpose

Use *before*, *during*, and *after* reading to

- Build vocabulary related to a particular instructional focus
- Help students develop analytical skills like classification and deduction
- Support students in their writing and other composing activities
- Build sight word reading fluency
- Provide a visual reference tool to help students remember important words related to a specific topic or focus

Directions

1. Create a list for a **Word Wall** that will help students deepen their vocabulary and enhance reading comprehension.

   Examples of word wall lists
   - Words connected to an upcoming unit of study
   - Words connected to specific instructional areas (e.g., math order of operations, historical terms, literary devices)
   - Difficult words found in textbook chapter
   - Words connected to a theme, book, or author
   - Related root words with different prefixes and affixes

2. Refer to the **Word Wall** throughout the unit of study about the content concept it relates to, being sure that students are actively interacting with the words on the wall.

   Examples of interactive activities
   - Sort the words into categories and label them (list-group-label or word sort)
   - Use 3–5 words on the wall to write a summary sentence about a main concept
   - Create an analytical graphic organizer that relates the words to one another
   - Write a narrative piece—short story, poem, description—that links several words on the **Word Wall** together in a meaningful way
   - Create a word game using the words on the wall—a crossword puzzle, word search, paired compare/contrast

Extensions

- Have students keep a **Triple-Entry Vocabulary Journal** with terms on the **Word Wall**.
- Have students create slide shows or visual presentations about the words on the wall.

Interactive Word Wall Planning Template

Name _____   Date _____

Directions

Think about the key ideas and concepts that will be covered in the textbook, other readings, or class instruction or discussion. Think of a way you could use an interactive word wall to deepen students' understanding of vocabulary and course concepts. Define the learning purposes, some sample words, and three activities you could do to have students interact with the words.

Word Wall concept _____

Learning purpose _____

Initial word list (will be added to during unit)

_____   _____

_____   _____

_____   _____

Interactive activity #1

Interactive activity #2

Interactive activity #3

Interactive Word Wall Content Sample

English Language Arts

During and *after* reading and writing descriptive essays

As students read exemplary descriptive essays, create a Word Wall of adjectives that create vivid word pictures.

Have students interact with the words by

- Identifying them during reading and discussing how they create reader interest.
- Revising a non-descriptive essay to a descriptive one by adding colorful, specific adjectives from the **Word Wall**.
- Creating an original piece using at least 15 adjectives from the **Word Wall**.
- Editing each others' descriptive essay drafts to provide feedback about adding adjectives to create visual imagery.

Mathematics

Before reading a text chapter on probability and solving problems related to coin and die tossing

Have students quickly peruse the chapter to identify what they think will be key terms related to probability e.g., *variable, distribution, reference class, set of possible values, experiment, outcome, event, sample space, probability of an event*.

Have students create their own **Triple-Entry Vocabulary Journal** entries about each word on the wall that includes a definition in their own words and a visual memory aid.

Have students interact with **Word Wall** terms by

- Arranging and rearranging the words to demonstrate the conceptual connections between the words.
- Adding terms to the **Word Wall** that amplify or clarify the terms.
- Writing a short persuasive essay on the importance of understanding mathematical probability, related to three or more Word Wall terms.

Science

Before, during, and *after* reading articles in a computer technology course about the new "thinking" technology called the Semantic Web

As the class reads articles about the Semantic Web, have students create a Word Wall with important terms, such as search engine, algorithms, relational database, RDF, GPS, logic engine, DNA computer, cubits, and quantum computing.

Have students interact with these words by

- Creating **Triple-Entry Vocabulary Journal** entries about each word on the wall that include a definition in their own words and a visual memory aid.
- Writing a short **Quick Write** defining the Semantic Web, using at least nine terms from the Word Wall.
- Drawing a Venn diagram that compares the World Wide Web and Semantic Web using **Word Wall** terms.

Social Studies

During and *after* reading a chapter on the ways production, distribution, and consumption differ in various countries in a economics class

As students read about these systems, have them create **Word Wall** cards and post them under one of the three categories on the wall: production, distribution, and consumption.

Have students interact with these words by

- Scrambling the words on the wall and asking students to list and group the words into the three systems of production, distribution, and consumption.
- Having students select a country they have studied and pick one word from each of the three systems that best represents that country's systems of production, distribution, and consumption.
- Having students select a word from the wall and do a short charade or role play, while other students guess the word.

Ideas for Increasing Student Interaction with Word Walls

Now that you've identified the important content area vocabulary words for your upcoming unit and you've decided how you'll display them in the room, what's next? How can you get your students to engage with the words on the **Word Wall** in ways that 1) don't take up all of your class time, 2) provide students with multiple exposures to the vocabulary, and 3) include approaches based on effective vocabulary instruction? The goal is to build a culture of using technical terms correctly (for the context), descriptively (to communicate), analytically (to diagnose and problem solve), and functionally (when they complete tasks). The following are some ideas to get you started—you can probably think of many more!

When students are reading textbooks, manuals, articles, etc.

- Provide points for finding/noticing **Word Wall** words in written material.
- Have students note where specific **Word Wall** words are found in print materials and add this information to the Word Wall. Students can compete in teams.
- Have students create definitions of **Word Wall** words as they read and then play matching games in the beginning of class for review or vote on the best definitions.
- Provide points if students suggest additional words for the **Word Wall** and can make a case for why the words are important to the unit of study.
- Have students mark present and past **Word Wall** words (as well as unfamiliar terms they encounter) when reading by underlining, using post-it notes, highlighting, etc.

When students are writing work summaries, logs, descriptions of how to complete certain processes, or quick writes/checks for understanding.

- Require the use of Word Wall words (2–3) in work reports, summaries, etc.
- Require all Word Wall terms be spelled correctly (since they are on the wall).
- Have students use Word Wall words in **Quick Writes** (for example, write down your two favorite words from the Word Wall and say why you like them; select two words from the Word Wall and describe how they are connected; write down everything you know about _____; compare and contrast two terms).

When students are talking/presenting about a topic or demonstrating how to do something.

- Expect that **Word Wall** words be used to complete the assignment. Require presentations use a certain number correctly.
- Have students "catch" other students using correct terminology.
- Post Word Walls in the classroom.
- Give points when students use **Word Wall** terms correctly when presenting/demonstrating.
- Make connections between **Word Wall** words and the topic at hand.
- Ask students to give synonyms, antonyms, examples, and non-examples when they use a word from the **Word Wall**.

Simple games students can play to learn the technical terms.

- Play games with the **Word Wall** words such as "slap" (provide a definition and the first one to slap the definition with a flyswatter wins).
- Play Jeopardy (What is…?), "I'm thinking of," or charades with **Word Wall** words.

When students are discussing a topic in class, first learning about a topic, reviewing the unit for a test.

- Have students complete a **Knowledge Rating Guide** with the words—ask the students to list the words under the appropriate heading: words they know and can explain, words they have heard of but are unsure what they mean, and words they have never heard of. Then discuss the words as a class.

- Ask students to list words from the **Word Wall** in a **Triple-Entry Vocabulary Journal** (word in context = 1st column; definition in own words = 2nd column; picture or way to remember the meaning of the word = 3rd column).

- Develop quadrant cards or **Frayer Models** for key concepts where students write the word in the center and give the definition, an example, a non-example, and a picture of the word.

- Have students do **Word Sorts** in pairs where students work together to put Word Wall words into categories.

- Have students complete a **Concept Map** or **Semantic Feature Analysis** using the Word Wall words as they complete the unit.

 **Caution!**

For most students...

Writing a word and its definition is not an effective way to learn vocabulary. Students tend to write down the first or shortest definition and to do this as a "compliance assignment," not as a way to learn technical vocabulary. To learn technical terms, students need multiple repetitions in multiple contexts, and to actively process the words (using a **Knowledge Rating Guide**, writing how two terms are connected, drawing a picture, giving examples and non-examples, playing games, etc.).

For many students...

Flashcards can be effective for review but not as a way to "learn" words. Have students interact with the **Word Wall** words in many ways before using flashcards.

For all students...

A glossary list or definitions sheet is not a Word Wall. Word Walls are public displays of words designed to support all students' reading, writing, and learning about a topic. Students can (and should!) make their own personal vocabulary lists, flashcard stacks, or **Triple-Entry Vocabulary Journals**, but that should be in addition to the **Word Wall**.

Chapter Preview/Tour

Description

A guided tour of the chapter about to be read that asks students to answer brief questions and make predictions related to chapter headings, vocabulary, text structure, and graphics.

Purpose

Use *before* reading to

- Provide an introduction to the text that will be read
- Help students make connections by linking text information with their own knowledge
- Identify how the text structure signals ideas and concepts
- Draw students' attention to text features
- Help students learn to use reading aids provided within the text

Directions

1. Model how to complete the **Chapter/Preview Tour** template.
2. Initially give students guidance in what to look for, e.g., bold vocabulary words, main ideas, broad concepts, text structure, important details, writing style, tone/mood, and themes.
3. Let students work collaboratively to preview text, complete a template, and share their ideas back to the whole class.
4. Have students complete **Chapter/Preview Tour** independently.

Extensions

- Have students describe in writing how the use of various text features helped them construct meaning from the text.
- Modify the template, ask students to work with you to collaboratively modify the **Chapter/Preview Tour** template to match different types of text (journal article, Web site text, chapter in a novel).

Chapter Preview/Tour Template

Name _____   Date _____

Directions

As you look through the assigned chapter, respond to the prompts below.

Textbook	

Reading Assignment Chapter _____ Pages _____

1. What is the title of the chapter?
    _____

    Create a question from the title.
    _____

2. List two headings or subheadings. Write a question for each.

    Heading _____

    Question _____

    Heading _____

    Question _____

3. Based on the *Introduction*, what will the chapter be about?
    _____
    _____

    Based on the *Summary,* list two important ideas in the chapter.

    a. _____

    b. _____

Chapter Preview/Tour Template (continued)

Textbook	

4. List two important vocabulary words.

   a. _____

   b. _____

   How do they appear in the text?

   _____

   _____

5. What kind of information do you get from words, phrases, or sentences in special type?

   _____

   _____

   List two important terms or ideas pointed out in special type.

   a. _____

   b. _____

6. What types of visuals do they have in the chapter (charts, graphs, pictures, maps, etc.)?

   _____

   List two important facts you learn from these visuals.

   a. _____

   b. _____

7. Based on your review, list the facts you already know about the topic of this chapter

This resource was developed by Roz Weizer. Used with permission.

Chapter Preview Content Examples

English Language Arts

Before and *after* reading a textbook section about magical realism

Build background knowledge about magical realism by reading a short excerpt from *100 Years of Solitude* and *The Bluest Eye*. Give students a **Chapter Preview** Template modified for fiction.

Model how to fill out the template and have students complete the template in partners before reading the section.

After students have read, review the information gathered as a class and discuss which information pertains to the two excerpts students listened to at the beginning of the lesson.

Mathematics

Before reading a textbook section unit on factors and multiples

Provide an introduction to the unit by identifying the "big ideas," which include determining factors; generating multiples; determining factorizations, including prime factorization of whole numbers.

Connect this to prior student learning about skip counting, multiplication and division facts and testing divisibility rules.

Have the students work in pairs to preview the unit and complete the modified template. Have each group share to the whole class their findings and one fact they already know about factors and multiples.

Science

Before reading an article or website about a topic

Explicitly teach students to navigate the resource, noticing, and becoming acquainted with standard text features such as sidebars with factual notes, captions, labels, TOCs, and indexes.

Modify the **Chapter Preview** template for each new text type and create prompts about concepts from your current science unit that challenge students to stop, think and record specific ideas or questions related to what they are studying.

Social Studies

Before reading a chapter on the westward expansion, have students work in groups of three to complete a **Chapter Preview** and then identify questions they have about the westward movement and American West in the 1800s.

List the questions and then have the groups read through the chapter and also review several websites such as http://www.pbs.org/weta/thewest/ and http://www.americanwest.com/ to find answers to the lists of questions generated by the groups.

Then complete a class **KWL Plus** chart that indicates what the class now knows and wants to learn in preparation for selection of individual research projects on the topic.

Anticipation/Reaction Guide

Description

A questioning strategy that assesses prior knowledge and assumptions at the pre-reading stage and evaluates the acquisition of concepts and use of supporting evidence after reading (Herber, 1978; Duffelmeyer & Baum, 1992).

Purpose

Use *before*, *during*, and *after* reading to

- Forecast and cue major concepts in the text to be read
- Motivate students to want to read text to see if prior knowledge is confirmed or disproved
- Require students to make predictions
- Activate students' existing background knowledge and set purpose for reading text
- Focus readers on the main ideas presented in text
- Help readers assess for misconceptions and reader-text discrepancies
- Create active interaction between reader and text
- Provide pre- and post-assessment information

Directions

1. Identify the important ideas and concepts students should focus on when reading.
2. Create 4–6 statements that support or challenge students' beliefs, experiences, and pre-existing ideas about the topic. The statement should be reasonably answered either way.
3. Set up a table for student responses like the template.

Sample Anticipation Reaction Guide *before* and *after* reading an article on healthy food

BEFORE READING				AFTER READING	
Agree	Disagree	Statement	Page(s) where evidence found	Agree	Disagree
		Diet soda is better for you than soft drinks with sugar.			
		Pasta is healthy for you.			
		Chocolate is bad for your teeth.			

4. *Before* reading the text, have students react to each statement in the *Before Reading* column individually and be prepared to support their position.
5. In small groups or as a whole class discussion, ask students to explain their initial responses to each statement.
6. Ask students to read the selection to find evidence that supports or rejects each statement.
7. *After* reading the text, ask students to react to each statement in the *After Reading* column to determine if they have changed their minds about any of the statements.

Extensions

- Have students use additional sources of information to support opinions.
- Ask students to rewrite any false statements based on the reading, individually or in cooperative groups.

Anticipation/Reaction Guide Template

Name _____   Date _____

BEFORE READING				AFTER READING	
Agree	Disagree	Statement	Pages where evidence found	Agree	Disagree
Conclusion(s)					

Anticipation/Reaction Guide Content Examples

English Language Arts

Before, during, and *after* reading *Romeo and Juliet*

Have students anticipate and react to the text, using the response headings of *Agree/Disagree*, including statements such as

- Romeo is a foolish character.

- Romeo and Juliet can be read as a comedy.

- The events that take place in *Romeo and Juliet* could happen today.

Mathematics

Before, during, and *after* reading a math textbook chapter on percents

Have students anticipate and react to the text, using the response headings of *True/False*, including statements such as

- A 20% off sale is better than a buy one-get one free sale.

- A mortgage of $1000 at 5% for 30 years is more expensive to pay off than $1000 at 7% for 30 years.

Science

Before, during, and *after* reading a global warming report issued by international scientists

Have students anticipate and react to the text, using the response headings of *Supported by Evidence/Not Supported by Evidence*, including statements such as

- Increasingly hotter temperatures around the globe show global warming is occurring.

- Hurricanes will continue to increase in frequency, especially in southern locations.

- Human causes are the leading reason for global warming.

Social Studies

Before, during, and *after* reading an informational Web site on voting

Have students anticipate and react to the text, using the response headings of *Accurate/Misrepresentation*, including statements such as

- More people voted for Independents in 2008 than in 2004.

- More people switched parties in the 2008 election than in the previous four elections.

Use of *Triple-Entry Vocabulary Journal* in a High School Science Classroom

Ms. Pritchett knew her students were experiencing difficulty understanding the vocabulary of the biology text. She tried asking the students to maintain a vocabulary notebook with the glossary definitions of the biology terms, but they were not successful on tests and could not seem to explain some of the science processes they had studied. How could she better help students connect vocabulary with understanding of science concepts? She knew it must move beyond memorization and writing of definitions. She decided to use the **Triple-Entry Vocabulary Journal** because it would give students the opportunity to develop a personal definition based on their understanding of the word used in context, along with representative diagrams and connections to each term.

Before Reading/Learning

Ms. Pritchett began the class by taking a large mass of dough and slowly stretching it apart at the center until it formed two new balls of dough. She asked the students, "What just happened?"

Josh raised his hand. "You just made two balls out of one?"

"Today we will begin a biology process that does something similar. We will learn about a process called *mitosis* and begin to understand the phases of *mitosis* by exploring the meaning of the terms or vocabulary."

"Before we look at the vocabulary, let's take a look at a brief animation of *Animal Cell Mitosis*." Afterwards, Ms. Pritchett asked Martin what he observed during the animation.

Martin shrugged and said, "I saw a bunch of squiggly things moving apart and dividing."

Ms. Pritchett said, "Exactly," and wrote his observation on the white board.

"Now, let's carry this further by breaking it down into sequences or phases. What did you see happening at the beginning of the animation?"

Billy volunteered an observation: "There was a single object that began to stretch apart."

"Great! Did you see any similarity to the ball of dough?" Several students nodded their head. Ms.

Pritchett wrote Billy's observation on the white board. "What else did you notice?"

Mary said, "It looked as though the further the ball stretched, the thinner it got in the center." Ms. Pritchett jotted the observation down.

Johnson said, "When it stretched really far, the ball actually divided and formed two new balls that looked exactly the same, just smaller." Ms. Pritchett recorded the last observation.

Ms. Pritchett said, "Before we begin our study of *mitosis*, we need to work with the vocabulary so that you can understand what you will be reading and learning about this topic." She handed out a template for the Triple-Entry Vocabulary Journal, which had three columns labeled *Word in Context, Definition in My Own Words,* and *Picture, Memory Aid, Phrase.* "We will be using this journal format today to help you as you record and learn new vocabulary related to cell division. Let's start with the word *mitosis.*"

"Turn in your book to the section on *mitosis*. Listen as I read the definition aloud, *Mitosis is the process in which a cell duplicates its chromosomes to generate two identical cells.* Hmmm," Ms. Pritchett said as she thought aloud. "I think duplicate means making a copy of something, like making a copy of a picture on a copier. So I know *mitosis* has something to do with making copies of chromosomes before it actually generates, or makes, two new cells." Using the white board, Ms. Pritchett modeled how to write the use of the word in context by including the phrase in which it is found and the page number. "But, I want a simpler definition I can understand. What do you think about this one? *Mitosis happens when a cell divides perfectly to form two new cells that are exactly alike.*" Several students nodded.

Scott said, "Yeah—that sounds right." So she wrote her own definition in the middle column, *Definition in My Own Words.*

"Okay, in the last column, I want to give an example or put in a visual that will help me remember the meaning of the word. For *mitosis*, I am going to connect it with the bread dough, which I divided into two identical balls. You can draw a picture, use clip art, include an example, or draw a diagram— whatever you think will help you to remember the definition."

"Before you begin working with a partner, I'd like you to look at the words connected with the phases of *mitosis*." She projected a Word Splash visual using WordArt of six vocabulary words, *interphase, prophase, metaphase, anaphase, telophase,* and *cytokinesis.* She pronounced each of the words and then asked the students to scan the text to locate the words. She reminded the students to record the page number next to the words so they could easily return to the word in the text as they worked to complete the vocabulary study.

During Reading/Learning

Ms. Pritchett knew the vocabulary might serve as a stumbling block for many students, so she decided to read the initial section of the text aloud, pausing to let students reread sentences that included one of the vocabulary words. She also provided time for students to think and talk about the word and make any notes or ask questions.

When she finished reading the introductory section aloud, Ms. Pritchett wanted to be sure each student understood how to use the Triple-Entry Vocabulary Journal before they began to work with a partner on the rest of the *mitosis* vocabulary. The class worked with the first two words as a large group. She asked each student to individually record the context meaning of *interphase* and write the meaning in their own words. She asked one or two students to share their personal definitions. Ms. Pritchett said, "I'm not looking for a Rembrandt. I only want the diagram to have meaning to you so you can remember the word." She guided the students as a class to complete the same process with *prophase.*

Ms. Pritchett continued the lesson by asking the students to work with a partner to read over the text together once more. She suggested looking for context clues in the surrounding sentences, captions, charts, and diagrams.

"But what if there isn't a clue?" asked Allie. "If you do not feel as though you have enough information, turn to the glossary to read a complete definition. Once you feel confident, you understand the meaning of the word, close the book, and discuss your definition with your partner before writing your own definition in column two. Then, in column three, draw a diagram of the phase of *mitosis* or write some personal connection with the phase. The goal is to create an aid to help jog

your memory so you will clearly understand and remember the meaning of the word."

Ms. Pritchett circulated the room to provide assistance as needed. She reminded several students to be precise when paraphrasing the text definitions. She noticed that two students seemed to be struggling with how to complete the assignment so she provided more explicit instruction on how to find the words and write their own definitions.

To help students develop a deeper understanding of the phases of *mitosis*, Ms. Pritchett had set up different stations in the lab using the microscopes and prepared slides to demonstrate the different phases of *mitosis.* The stations were purposely randomly arranged and not labeled as to the phases of *mitosis.* She asked the students to move as groups of four to view the slides and to identify the correct labels and order for the six phases. She asked them to add information they observed in the third column of their Triple-Entry Vocabulary Journal if it added to their understanding of that particular phase.

After Reading/Learning

To determine the level of student understanding, Ms. Pritchett asked the students to complete a **Quick Write** to explain the sequence of divisions, or phases, the cell moves through to form two daughter cells from one parent cell. She gave the students a moment to reflect and think about the vocabulary, animation, and slides they had worked with during class, and encouraged them to use the information from their Triple-Entry Vocabulary Journals. She stressed the purpose of the Quick Write is not to test them, but to give them another way to practice using the vocabulary and think about the concept of *mitosis.* It was encouraging to see that almost all of the students were writing, since this was not always the case. She knew that some students would need additional support to use the Triple-Entry Vocabulary Journal, but she felt the engagement of the students during today's lesson indicated a positive connection with the strategy and learning new vocabulary. She resolved to ask the students if they found the strategy helpful when class met the next day.

Part 3: Building New Knowledge

Part 3: Building New Knowledge

Introduction

In the classroom, we often introduce content and then ask students to read, learn and communicate their learning in some way. But, when students are assigned reading rather than given support to actively engage with the text, they tend to do just enough to meet the requirements of the assignment. Having work to complete *after* reading is not motivating enough to get students to actively engage with reading. Often this is because students do not have the habit of engaging with the text and/or the skills to engage with the text, especially if the text is challenging.

The tools in this section of the Toolkit, Building New Knowledge, were selected so that you can help students develop the habits of engaging and making meaning of text. Many of the tools relate to notetaking and organizing content for future use. These are skills that many students need help to develop. You will find a selection of student learning strategies, teacher instructional practices, and collaborative routines designed to help students interact with vocabulary and text during reading and learning. Many of these tools can also be used to support writing and discussion activities after reading and learning.

In this section of the Toolkit, you will find the following approaches to supporting reading and learning:

	Reading & Learning Phases		
	Before	During	After
Student Learning Strategies			
Analytic Graphic Organizers		✓	✓
Semantic Feature Analysis – all content areas	✓	✓	✓
Discussion Web – Social Studies		✓	✓
Proposition/Support Outline – Science and Social Studies	✓	✓	✓
Inference Notes Wheel – English Language Arts		✓	✓
Five-Step Problem Solving Organizer – Mathematic		✓	✓
Question-Answer Relationship (QAR)		✓	
Coding/Comprehension Monitoring		✓	
Two-Column Note Taking		✓	✓
Question the Author (QtA)		✓	
Collaborative Routines			
Think-Pair-Share	✓	✓	✓
Reciprocal Teaching		✓	
Paired Reading		✓	
Classroom Scenarios			
Use of *Analytic Graphic Organizer* and *Interactive Word Wall* in a Middle School Mathematics Classroom		✓	✓
Use of *Coding/Comprehension Monitoring* in an Elementary Social Studies Classroom		✓	

Question-Answer Relationship (QAR)

Description

This strategy involves students in assessing the thinking demands of a passage and developing answers for four types of questions: *right there* (answer is directly stated in text); *think and search* (answer is in the text, but not stated directly); *author and me* (the answer is not in the text but is derived from integrating the author's information with one's own background knowledge and experiences); and *on my own* (the answer is not in the text; the reader must develop the answers solely from background knowledge) (Raphael, 1982, 1984).

Purpose

Use *during* reading to
- Characterize questions and know how to construct the answers using the text, where applicable
- Become more analytical and evaluative about responding to questions
- Separate factual, implied, inferred, and predictive information while reading
- Determine the supporting evidence for responses to questions

Directions

1. Prepare a sample text reading with several questions that correspond to the four **QAR** types.
2. Explain that this strategy helps readers determine how to seek answers for questions about the text.
3. Show students the four types of **QAR** questions.

Right there	*Think and search*
The answer is stated directly in the text.	The answer is in the text but not stated directly. The reader interprets the meaning from different parts of the text.
Author and me	*On my own*
The answer is not in the text. The reader must read the text in order to answer, but must use personal knowledge with the information provided by the author.	The answer is not in the text. The reader must develop the answer based on knowledge and personal experience only.

4. Introduce several examples of *right there* questions, then introduce several *think and search* questions. Emphasize that both types of questions require locating information within the text.
5. Introduce several *author and me* and *on my own* questions for the same text reading.
6. Provide guided practice in small groups with several progressively longer pieces of text.
7. As students become more proficient, provide independent practice and give feedback to individual students about their **QAR** choices.
8. Once students can effectively use **QAR** to answer questions, have them generate their own questions to practice the various types and use **QAR** independently.

Extension

Link the **QAR** types of questions to **Critical Thinking Cue Questions**: *right there* to knowledge; *think and search* to comprehension and application; *author and me* to analysis; and *on my own* to evaluation and synthesis.

Question-Answer Relationship (QAR) Content Examples

Mathematics

Elementary School

Use **QAR** to help students figure out if they need to use the glossary or go back to an earlier part of the chapter.

Example of teacher introduction of **QAR**, using guided questions.

Teacher:	What is a fraction?
Student:	It says it is a name for part of a whole.
Teacher:	Yes, the answer is in the book. It's a *right there* question. But what about this statement, *you name fractions by their numerators and denominators*. What do these words mean?
Student:	It doesn't say.
Teacher:	Look around the entire page. Can you see the definition anywhere?
Student:	Yes, it's in a box on the next page.
Teacher:	So sometimes you have to *think and search* to find an answer. That's another type of question, *think and search*. But what if the words weren't defined in that box?
Student:	I'd have to look it up?
Teacher:	Yes, you'd be on your own to learn it or you'd use hints from the book plus what you already know to figure it out. Sometimes you figure out and answer from the author and your own mind. That's called *author and me* questions. Or, if no answer is in the book, that's called *on your own* questions because you have to find the answer without help from the book.

Middle School

Use a **QAR** during a Mathscape lesson on nets that catch cubes to help students understand they must read the text, analyze the graphics, and use their own knowledge to figure out the math. After explaining the four types of **QAR** questions, show them a completed **QAR** chart with both the question and the answer in the four quadrants.

Right there	*Think and search*
What is a net? It says right in the text that it is "a 2-D figure that can be folded on its segments or curved on its boundaries to form a 3-D shape."	What happens when I change the dimensions to the shape? How is it different for a two dimensional shape vs. a three dimensional shape? I have to use the computer application and the text to get the answer.
Author and me	*On my own*
What is a three dimensional shape? I know from the picture that it's like a box. I know from my own experience that a box has shape and isn't flat like it looks on the page. So I can guess that dimension means a shape that isn't flat.	How many different nets can there be for a cube? Nothing in these pictures show me the answer. The text doesn't tell me either. I'd have to draw it or look it up in another book.

High School

Before, *during*, and *after* reading a variety of data charts and graphs, use **QAR** to help students determine if the answer is provided in the data display or whether analysis, manipulation, computation, or calculation is needed to respond to the different kinds of questions.

Teacher-generated responses to model **QAR** for data analysis

Right there	*Think and search*
The specific number is provided.	The answer is there, but I need to understand the structure of the chart to locate the answer.
Author and me I can figure out the answer from the data if I do some calculations.	*On my own* The data doesn't provide a specific answer. I have to manipulate the data and figure it out on my own.

Science

Elementary School

When students are unsure how to do a science lab, help them understand when they must follow the lab directions or when they must think on their own by modifying the **QAR** cues they're already studied in reading.

Teacher-modified terms for the QAR in science

Right there	*Think and search*
The directions tell me to do it.	I have to read the directions and also look at the illustrations.
Author and me I have to follow the directions, but I also need to know what the words mean.	*On my own* When the lab question says, *what do you think*, it's a cue that I have to figure it out. The answer won't be in the book.

Middle School

While preparing students for the new state test in science, help them understand the different kinds of questions that may be on the test and how to select the multiple choice answer.

Teacher-designed cues for using **QAR** question types to analyze test questions

Right there	*Think and search*
Does the question ask for just one fact? It's probably a right there question.	Does the question ask you to choose several answers? It's probably a think and search question.
Author and me Does the question ask about something the text doesn't fully explain? You will need to add your own knowledge to what the author has said.	*On my own* Is the question a prompt that asks what you think? Then you have to form an opinion and support it with information from the passage.

High School

After reading a variety of articles on global warming, have students who already know **QAR** create their own questions. Provide a set of cue words to help them analyze the facts and opinions in the articles in their discussion groups.

Teacher-created cue words to guide students in generating **QAR** questions

Right there Who, where, list, when, how many, name, what, based on this passage	*Think and search* Summarize, what caused, contrast, explain, retell, how did, find
Author and me In what instances?	*On my own* If you were this person, what would you think based on your experience? You have to form an opinion and support it with information from the passage.

Social Studies

Elementary School

During reading of a nonfiction book about Harriet Tubman, have students answer questions and write them in the **QAR** quadrant that they used to figure it out.

Teacher-generated questions

Right there What made Harriet very unhappy when she was a child?	*Think and search* Why didn't Harriet's husband go with her to Baltimore?
Author and me What caused Harriet's sleeping spells?	*On my own* What do you like or dislike about Harriet's husband John?

Student response to these questions

Right there It says on page 17 that he didn't go because he had gotten married again!	*Think and search* Her master took her mom and the children away from her dad. Later in the story, Harriett was taken away from her family. Then it said she was beaten for not cleaning the house right.
Author and me Harriett was hurt by an iron weight. Weeks later she had sleeping spells. My mom wasn't sick at first with her cancer, but it made her sick later. So I think the iron weight caused the sleeping spells.	*On my own* At first I liked him because he was a freeman who married a slave, so he wasn't prejudiced. But later he married someone else and ditched Harriet. He didn't ask for a divorce, he just married someone else.

Middle School

When students struggle with map interpretation, help them apply the **Question-Answer Relationship** strategy they use in reading text to study of the map.

Teacher application of **QAR** types to maps

Right there The answer is on the map, such as a name of a city.	**Think and search** The answer is partly on the map, but you must use the map key to understand what the symbol or color means.
Author and me The answer is on the map, but you have to understand what the vocabulary means to answer the question.	**On my own** There is nothing in the map or map key that gives the answer. The answer is your opinion or what you already know.

High School

When students struggle to understand a complex world history textbook, check that they are using all the information in charts, sidebars, chapter summaries, and illustrations to understand the content.

Teacher explanation of text features

Right there Look for an answer that is directly stated in words.	**Think and search** Put the answer together, using the words, the pictures, and the charts.
Author and me Figure out the answer by combining what you already know with the information that is given.	**On my own** Nothing in the words, pictures, or charts tells the specific answer. You must form your own answer based on what you know and understand.

English Language Arts

Elementary School

When reading a short biography about Samuel Clemens, have students who have already used the **QAR** strategy several times develop their own **QAR** questions from the text.

Student example of **QAR** questions about Samuel Clemens

Right there Where and when was Samuel Clemens born?	**Think and search** What jobs did he have when he was a boy?
Author and me Why did Clemens write *Life on the Mississippi*?	**On my own** Why did you think he changed his name to Mark Twain?

Middle School

After reading a selection that is followed by comprehension questions, use QAR to help students understand whether the questions are literal or require analytical, evaluative, or inferential thinking.

Teacher generated questions to model **QAR** for *The Diary of Anne Frank*

Right there Who is in the house besides the Franks?	*Think and search* Who makes the rules, Mr. or Mrs. Frank?
Author and me Why is Anne rebellious?	*On my own* What would you have done differently from Anne?

High School

Introduce the **QAR** strategy with a visual, such as *The Scream* by Edward Munch. Model the thinking behind the four types of questions by having students explain how they figured out the answer and then telling them the **QAR** type (Raphael, T. E. 1982).

Teacher:	How many people are in this image?
Student:	Three men. The men are right there in the image.
Teacher:	This is a *right there* question. The answer is right there for you to see.
Teacher:	What is the setting in this image? How did you figure it out?
Student:	It's during the day, on a bridge, near the ocean or a river. I looked at different parts of the image.
Teacher:	This is a *think and search* question. It's in the image, but you have to look in several different places to figure out the entire answer.
Teacher:	Is the man in the foreground the protagonist/hero or is he the antagonist/victim?
Student:	He looks mean. I think he's the villain. I know a man who scowls like that and he's really mean. I used some clues from the image and what I already know to figure it out.
Teacher:	This is an *author and me* question. You use information in the image and in your own head to answer the question.
Teacher:	What kinds of things make a person scream?
Student:	My sister screams during scary movies. We don't know from this image why he is screaming, but I'd guess he's scared. Fear makes most people scream.
Teacher:	This is an *on my own* question. There is nothing in the image that answers the question. You have to use only what you know and answer the question on your own.

Coding/Comprehension Monitoring

Description

This strategy helps students to engage and interact with text and monitor comprehension as they read.

Purpose

Use *during* reading to

- Support content area learning by focusing on key concepts
- Provide a way for students to engage in a dialogue with the author
- Help students identify how they process information while reading
- Help students identify what is difficult in the text so they can select and apply comprehension strategies to support their reading
- Develop metacognitive awareness and ability to monitor one's own comprehension

Directions

1. Explain that this strategy helps readers monitor their reading so they can identify what they do or don't understand.
2. Choose 2–3 codes that support the purpose of the reading and reinforce targeted literacy habits and skills.
3. Model the strategy, using an overhead or whiteboard. Do a **Think-Aloud** while marking the codes so students witness the metacognitive process.
4. Guide the students to apply the coding strategy. Review the codes and have students code their reactions as they read on the page margins, lined paper inserts, or sticky notes.

Possible Codes (use only 2–4 codes per time)

+	New information	!	Interesting
*	I know this information	-->	Important information
?	I don't understand/I have questions	T-T	Text-to-text connection
P	Problem	T-W	Text-to-world connection
S	Solution	T-S	Text-to-self connection
✓	I agree	C	Cause
X	I disagree	E	Effect

Extensions

- Have students compare and discuss how they coded sections of the text.
- After students are comfortable with coding using teacher-provided codes, encourage them to develop additional codes appropriate for reading a particular text.

Coding/Comprehension Monitoring Template

Name _____   Date _____

Note: This template is useful if students cannot write in or mark the text directly and sticky notes are not available for use.

Page	Page	Page	Page	Page

Directions

Insert this sheet in your book behind the reading assignment. As you read each page, write the page number at the top of the column. Then place the code directly across from the part of the text you are coding. Each time you read a new page, pull out this sheet to the corresponding next page and add your codes.

Write down the 2–4 codes you will use to monitor your comprehension as you read the assignment.

__ = _____

__ = _____

__ = _____

__ = _____

Coding Content Examples

Mathematics

Elementary School

After reviewing addition, subtraction, multiplication, and division rules at the beginning of the school year, have students code a variety of written problems to find the cue words in the passage that tell them whether adding, subtracting, multiplying, or dividing is required to solve the problem.

Codes

A = addition
S = subtraction

M = multiplication
D = division

Middle School

Show students that coding of text is similar to coding of math problems. Explain that coding is a way to understand the patterns of written text, just like manipulatives are a physical code to help students see the patterns in mathematical problems. Model mathematical coding using the Lab Gear blocks in Mathscape's *Exploring the Unknown* lessons on writing and solving equations. Have them practice mathematical coding by using a set of blocks to illustrate a written expression, such as $x^2 + 5 + x = y^2$, followed by rearranging the blocks to combine like terms, $3x^2 + 2x + 5$.

Codes

Yellow blocks = constants

Blue blocks = variables

High School

While reviewing for the SATs, show students that coding is an effective way to determine how to carry out the operations in the correct order. Remind them of the acronym PEMDAS—Please Excuse My Dear Aunt Sally. Give a set of sample problems that require performing more than one operation and have them code the problems using PEMDAS.

Codes

P = parentheses
E = exponents

M & D = multiplication and divisions left to right
A & S = addition and subtraction from left to right

Science

Elementary School

During a lesson on the circulatory system, assess students' prior knowledge and current understanding by having them code in the margins of the handout.

Codes

! = I already know this information
? = I don't understand/I have questions

V = new vocabulary
X = I thought differently

Middle School

During a lesson on the reproduction of plants, introduce coding as a method to identify patterns and relationships in text the same way labels help you identify the patterns or relationships of a photograph or diagram. Using guided questioning, have students determine codes for an illustration of the life cycle of an apple: *pollination*, *fertilization*, *fruit development*, and *seed dispersal*.

Have them do online research in pairs to find articles about the reproduction of maples, lemons, peas, or tomatoes; print out the article and code the text for the stages of reproduction.

Codes

P = pollination
F = fertilization

D = fruit development
S = seed dispersal

High School

In a human anatomy and physiology class where coding has already been frequently used, have students skim and scan their independent reading handouts to identify key focus areas, define codes, and code the article in the margins. Use the coded assignments to confirm that assigned reading has been done and to monitor individual progress with text comprehension.

Directions to students: Skim the assigned reading. Determine the key types of information you will need to understand. Select 2–4 codes that will help you focus while you read. You may use any of the following codes or define your own codes.

Codes

V = new vocabulary
! = key information to remember
F = function
T = important theory
M = measurement or calculation

P = procedure
A = abnormality
S = sequence or cycle
C = cause
E = effect

Social Studies

Elementary School

Introduce coding with map study before teaching students how to code text. Have students review the maps of three different states and mark the codes on the laminated maps with washable markers. Then have students read in the text about the states they chose using the following codes.

Codes

C = capital city
H = historical events happened here

P = places of interest
W = name of large bodies of water in or bordering state

Middle School

While reading the text chapter on European explorers and the colonizing of North America, have students code both the text and the maps to identify which countries explored the different areas of North America.

Codes

P = Portugal
S = Spain
N = Netherlands

E = England
F = France

High School

When reading the Declaration of Independence, have students code the document in order to compare and make connections with the grievances of that time to today's world.

Codes

Y = yes, this grievance is still important today
N = no, this grievance is not as relevant today

X = I don't see why this was a problem then or now
? = I don't know if this grievance fits our society now

English Language Arts

Elementary School

In a unit about champions, model to students how to code the attributes of what it takes to be a champion, using a short article or story about an Olympic champion. Provide several articles about different kinds of champions in life, such as firefighters or scientists, for them to read and code in pairs using the same codes. Ask the librarian to put together a group of stories and online articles about champions in diverse occupations. Have students select their own text to practice coding independently, using the same codes to identify the attributes of a champion.

Codes

T = talent
D = dedication and determination

W = hard work and practice
! = passion to be the best

Middle School

During a poetry unit, help students understand the impact sound has on the reader by using coding to identify the techniques the poets use to achieve different sound effects. After teaching the elements of sound, have students work in pairs to code several poems. Reinforce student understanding of coding by having students independently practice coding with the same set of poems, using a second set of codes for figurative language.

Codes for sound

R = rhyme
M = meter

A = alliteration and assonance
O = onomatopoeia

Codes for figurative language

I = imagery
P = personification

S = simile
M = metaphor

High School

During a unit on analyzing essays, use coding to help students see how literacy devices and style conventions are used by authors to create interest or persuade readers to take their point of view. Select an engaging topic like environment. Model coding with an excerpt from Rachel Carson's *Silent Spring*. Then have students work in small groups to analyze four environmental essays that vary in style, length, and reading difficulty such as Benjamin Franklin's *The Whistle*, Annie Dillard's *In the Jungle*, E. B. White's *Cold Weather*, Harry Crews' *The Hawk Is Flying*, Edward Abbey's *Desert Images*, R. J. Heathorn's *Learn with BOOK*, or a longer essay from John McPhee's *Control of Nature*. Have students share devices they coded and explain how they contributed to the reader's understanding of the author's point of view.

Codes

I = information
D = description

P = persuasion
V = voice and word choice

Two-Column Note Taking

Description

The **Two-Column Note Taking** strategy can be used with text, lectures, or when viewing media presentations to help students organize their thinking about specific content. It is sometimes called a double-entry journal when used with fictional text or when the focus is on a student's personal response to the text instead of on "taking notes." When combined with a summary, it is often referred to as "Cornell Notes" (Pauk, 1962).

Purpose

Use *during* and *after* reading to

- Create a user-friendly system to record important ideas, related details, and the relationships between concepts
- Help students remember important points and deepen their understanding of content
- Help students organize information and thoughts for thinking, writing, studying, or presenting

Directions

1. Ask students to divide their paper into two columns.
2. Mark the columns with the appropriate headings.

Ideas for possible headings			
Fiction		**Nonfiction**	
Column 1	**Column 2**	**Column 1**	**Column 2**
Passage	Response	Main idea	Detail
Character	Decision	Cause	Effect
Quote	Importance	Concept	Example
		Issue	Connection to own life

3. Model how to do the following: In the left-hand column, write a sentence, quote, or cause from the selection along with the page number. In the right-hand column, write the definition, give an example, make a connection to your life, or list an effect.
4. Provide the specific words, quotes, etc., in the left-hand column that you want students to respond to or ask for detail about.
5. Have students complete two-column notes independently, making sure the headings fit the reading/purpose for reading.

Extensions

- Students share their responses with others and solicit feedback.
- Students can use two-column notes as study guides, support for writing essays/summaries, or to take notes from films or lectures.
- Ask students to write a summary based on the information in their notes.

Two-Column Note Taking Template

Name _____   Date _____

Directions

Fill in the appropriate headings that match your purpose for reading/listening. As you read/listen/view, take two-column notes about important facts, vocabulary, concepts, and other information you want to remember or will need to use.

Topic
Check one: Lecture ☐   Text ☐   Film ☐   Presentation/Demonstration ☐

© 2011 Public Consulting Group

Two-Column Note Taking Content Examples

Mathematics

Elementary School

When teaching estimating, have the students record their estimate in the left column before solving the problem, then write the exact answer in the right column. Comparing the two responses will help them understand if they are making good predictions when they estimate.

Example of student notes

Estimated answer to the problem	Correct answer to the problem
93 + 48 = estimated 90 + 50 = 140	93 + 48 = 141
1,859 − 997 = estimated 2000 − 1000 = 1000	1,859 − 997 = 862

Middle School

Over time, help students take two-column notes from the text readings, showing them how to change the headers according to the specific content.

Examples of teacher-selected headers

Formula	Definition and/or Example
Function	Graph
Problem	Factoring Process

High School

When reviewing how to simplify expressions with equivalent fractions, have students keep two-column notes for the examples used in class so they will have examples to review while doing homework.

Example of student notes

Algebraic expression	Simplified expression
$\dfrac{3a^2x}{6a}$	$\dfrac{ax}{2}$
$\dfrac{16\,ab^3c^2}{24ab^2c^5}$	$\dfrac{2b}{3c^3}$

Science

Elementary School

Help students learn to take two-column notes using a mix of text and graphics. As they read an illustrated article on environmental organisms, have them create a list of all the living and nonliving things mentioned.

Example of student notes

Biotic factors (living things)	Abiotic factors (nonliving things and factors)
Water lilies	Soil
Frogs	Light
Fish	Temperature

Middle School

After reading each text chapter and completing the related lab or applied task, have students keep a weekly journal to record their understanding of how science changes cause varied effects and reactions.

Example of student notes for *Heat Sources*

Cause	Effect/Reaction
Heating fluid in a closed container	Pressure builds up and the fluid boils over
Using a container that is not heat resistant	It may melt or crack when used over heat
Using tongs or test tube clamps	Prevents you from burning your fingers

High School

When studying states of matter in a beginning chemistry class, have students keep a two-column notes journal of examples and characteristics of each state.

Example of student notes

State of matter	Example and characteristics
Solid	Gold – holds its own shape, high density, and is not affected by pressure
Liquid	Water – adopts the shape of its container, high density, and not affected by pressure
Gas	Nitrogen – expands to fill its container, low density, and is affected by pressure
Plasma	Interior of the sun – exists only at high temperatures, low density, and depends on pressure

Social Studies

Elementary School

When introducing facts and opinions, create a **Two-Column Note Taking** chart to help students understand the difference. Have the students find two facts in the text selection, enter them, and create an opinion related to each fact. Have students find two opinions in the text, enter them, and create a fact statement related to each opinion.

Fact	Opinion

Middle School

During a world history unit, have students keep a reflection journal to summarize the contributions of famous people throughout history. Have them use their notes to write a report on the attributes and contributions that make a person's legacy stand the test of time.

Example of student notes

Historical Figure	Major contributions

High School

When studying the civil war, have students research and compare the American Civil War with a 20th or 21st century war to help them understand people's responses to war policy and tactics. As the small groups do their research, have them keep two-column notes that define the similarities or differences between the wars and how the nation responded to them.

Example of student notes

American Civil War	Vietnam War
Many Civil War battles were fought on battlefields that were out in the open and the battles themselves were two armies marching toward one another and clashing in the center of the field.	North Vietnamese soldiers used guerrilla warfare methods such as jungle warfare, and used women and children for war tasks. Americans were shocked by the guerrilla tactics.
Veterans on both sides were respected after the war, both immediately and long afterwards.	USA soldiers who fought in Vietnam were not given much respect after their return and fought for many years to be recognized.

English Language Arts

Elementary School

Help students begin to understand inferential thinking by using two-column note taking to identify characters' feelings and the clues from their words or behaviors that hint at them.

Example of student notes

Character's feelings (such as happy, angry, sad)	Clues that show how the character feels (such as words, appearance, or behavior)
Pierre is very frustrated.	He kicked the dirt after dropping the ball. He frowned when his coach said he'd get better with practice.
Tony is mean.	He laughed when Pierre dropped the ball.
The coach is understanding.	He encouraged Pierre. He didn't yell at him.

Middle School

During the study of the epic genre, have students use two-column note taking as they read excerpts from *The Odyssey* to help them understand how Odysseus' internal conflicts related to his external conflicts.

Example of student notes

Odysseus' internal conflicts	Odysseus' external conflict
He refused to run from Cyclops because he wanted to see the caveman.	His refusal got his men angry because they wanted to make a run for it.

High School

After reading a collection of short stories from South Africa, help students connect to very different life styles than they've experienced in the USA by responding to unique quotations.

Example of student notes for *Somehow Tenderness Survives: Stories of Southern Africa*, by Hazel Rochman

Quote and page number	Connection (This reminds me of) Question (I wonder...) Confusion (I don't understand)
"The cold went through my shirt and shorts." p. 9	I thought it was HOT in Africa!
"The white man stares till I lowered my eyes. Well, he said." p. 18	The white man demands respect from Les. But not from his own boys. Is it all about color?

Question the Author (QtA)

Description

This strategy asks students to pose questions that interpret and critique what the author is saying, engaging them to construct meaning beyond what the text explicitly states (Beck, McKeown, Hamilton, & Snapp, 1997).

Purpose

Use *during* reading to

- Engage students by deepening their thinking and problem solving while reading
- Enrich student discussions and interactions with text
- Support comprehension of difficult but important sections of text
- Develop metacognitive thinking to monitor and enhance comprehension

Directions

1. Introduce and discuss the topic of authorship.

2. Explicitly teach and discuss ideas related to authors' opinions and decision making about what to put in their writing, such as biographical information that indicates their perspective from their educational or work background, age, culture, or other demographic factors.

3. Discuss the potential strengths and fallibility of the author in terms of the currency of their knowledge base, their ability to communicate ideas and information, and their assumptions about the audience that reads their writing.

4. Select a text passage to model the **Question the Author** process with students, choosing pre-determined pause points where you will initiate discussion to clarify the author's writing. For example, share questions you would ask the author about the messages or informational clarity or assumptions about the audience's knowledge.

5. Have students generate questions that query the author's intentions, not the text information itself. Discuss what the author is trying to communicate. Continue this guided practice with a series of passages across several different texts until most students demonstrate capability of generating meaningful author queries.

6. Ask students to generate their own **Question the Author** questions during **Paired Reading**, then independent reading. Post a list of example questions to help them get started, while making clear your expectation that they should formulate their own questions as well.

   Examples of QtA queries

   - What is the author telling us (the reader)?
   - That is what the author wrote, but what is the author really saying?
   - What does the author want us to understand/know?
   - Does the author explain _____ clearly?
   - What prior knowledge about _____ does the author think the reader has?

Extension

- Combine **QtA** with other literacy support strategies like **Critical Thinking Cue Questions**, **Reciprocal Teaching**, or **Group Summarizing**.

Question the Author (QtA) Template

Name _____   Date _____

Reading Selection _____

Biographical information about the author

Your questions for the author

- What is the author telling us (the reader)?
- That is what the author wrote, but what is the author really saying?
- What does the author want us to understand/know?
- Does the author explain _____clearly?
- What prior knowledge about _____does the author think the reader has?

Your answers to these questions

Your conclusions about the author's writing

© 2011 Public Consulting Group

This resource was developed by Beck, McKeown, Hamilton, & Kugan, L. (1997).

Question the Author (QtA) Content Examples

English Language Arts

English Language Arts	Mathematics
Before and *during* reading of a new poetry form, have students use **Question the Author** as a way to investigate the poem's structure and writing style.	*During* a unit on statistics, provide students with two articles reporting polling results.
Have students pose and answer questions for the author about the number of words or syllables in a line, rhyme scheme, breaks, or literary techniques.	After analyzing the statistics and graphs presented, ask students to use **QtA** to discuss why the two authors of the articles may have represented the statistics in different ways, what the bias or perspective of each author might be, and how that might have influenced the narrative of the article.
Then, as a class, use the answers to students' questions to build a concept map of the features of that particular form of poetry.	Discuss how the math could be represented differently to emphasize different points.
Science	**Social Studies**
Provide students with readings that represent two different theories on the reason for the mass extinction that wiped out dinosaurs.	*During* a unit on the Civil War, provide students with a variety of primary source documents about a single battle or issue.
Use **QtA** to engage students in a consideration of the differences among scientific points of view for this topic.	Working in pairs, students can use **QtA** to identify the various points of view represented and then use a graphic organizer to record the key ideas.
Divide students into two groups and give one reading to each. Ask each group to use **QtA** and record answers to their questions on chart paper.	Have students discuss why these points of view are different. Then ask students to read a section on the same event in a textbook and identify which of the points of view in the primary source documents are represented, or are missing. Discuss why this might be the case.
Then have the two groups switch articles and repeat the exercise. Use the chart paper responses to engage students in a debate on the issue.	

About Analytic Graphic Organizers

Why Use Analytic Graphic Organizers?

Current research in learning and brain development confirms what visual learners intuitively understand: Organizing information visually creates new connections to content (Clarke, 1991). It facilitates the development of deeper and more complex schema by structuring information in non-linear ways. For instance, think about how difficult it would be to teach the location of all the states in the U.S. without using a map (Hyerle, 1996)! Although linear representations (like outlines) are very useful in certain contexts, visual consideration, representation, and organization of information allows us to think about things in more elegant, interconnected ways.

What does this mean for you? Helping your students develop proficiency with the use of **Analytic Graphic Organizers** can help them to develop a more sophisticated understanding of text structures and purposes than they may be able to achieve alone. This is great news for you as a teacher because it means that you have a collection of powerful visual tools at your disposal to help your students build background knowledge, develop new information, and extend learning.

Strategy or Worksheet? How to Use Analytic Graphic Organizers

Although **Analytic Graphic Organizers** (AGOs) are extremely useful tools, their usefulness is entirely determined by a single person in your classroom: you. How you select, teach, and support the use of an AGO can result in a powerful learning experience for your students or can end up as an exercise in filling in boxes. The power of the **Analytic Graphic Organizer** will be maximized if you take these steps:

Define the learning goals for the lesson you are teaching. What are you trying to teach students to do? What learning skills do you want them to develop? Think about what you are trying to accomplish in the lesson, both in terms of content and academic knowledge. This will help you select the appropriate AGO for the lesson.

Analyze the cognitive demands of the text you want students to read. What sort of structure does it have? What is its purpose? What is likely to be difficult about it? Very few of us would purchase software for our computer without thinking about how easy it will be to use. These days, we apply this mindset to everything from cars to cereal. Look at the text you are using for your lesson with this same analytical eye.

Match the goals and demands to the AGO. If you want students to develop the capacity to compare and contrast, using the Brainstorming Web will likely be less effective than a **Semantic Feature Analysis** or a Venn diagram.

Use the Gradual Release Model. This model will help you to teach students how to really use the AGO effectively. Use **Think-Alouds** to model for students what sort of thinking you do when you are trying to make sense of information.

*Use the **Analytic Graphic Organizer** once it is filled out.* Don't make the mistake of having students "fill it out and hand it in." Because so much learning depends on metacognition, think about ways for students to interact with the organizer in multiple ways. Have your students share information with each other, complete AGOs in pairs, or create a class AGO for a difficult concept. Bring the organizer out for multiple lessons throughout a unit and challenge your students to make additions or changes.

When to Use Analytic Graphic Organizers

Although the AGOs in this book are listed primarily in this *Building New Knowledge* section, you will also find that graphic organizers throughout the *Thinkquiry Toolkit*. Below are some ideas for how you might use AGOs before, during, and after reading to help your students learn more effectively.

Before Reading

1. Use a **KWL Plus** chart to build background knowledge and set learning goals.
2. Have students create a collective **Concept Map** for an upcoming unit. As the unit progresses, have them add or change the map to reflect their new learning.
3. Have students begin a **Triple-Entry Journal** by skimming a new text for words they don't know.

During Reading

1. Use an organizer matched to the structure of the text students are reading to help them pull out critical information.
2. Once students become familiar with AGOs that focus on text structure, provide a variety of organizers to students and challenge them to look at a text and figure out which AGO is the best one to use to organize the information.
3. Use **Discussion Webs** to help students develop academic distance from controversial topics. Have students fill out both sides of the web and exchange papers with a partner. The goal should be for the partner to be unable to tell which point of view the student holds.
4. Use **Semantic Feature Analysis** or Venn diagram to help students visualize shared and unique characteristics among two or more concepts in a text.

After Reading

1. Use the **KWL Plus** as a way to have students review information and think about what they have learned.
2. Have students fill out the other side of a **Discussion Web**.
3. Put students in groups to fill out collective **Concept Maps** that represent their understanding of an idea after they have read. Have students share their thinking with others and discuss which organizational structure best represents the content.

Analytic Graphic Organizers

Description

This strategy uses a visual format like charts, diagrams, and graphs to help students explore the characteristics, relationships, or effects of a complex topic. This supports students to organize their thoughts and construct meaning from text. Examples include cause-effect diagrams, comparison-contrast charts, and process flow diagrams.

Purpose

Use *during* and *after* reading to

- Provide a visual way to analyze how information and ideas are linked
- Help organize information for note-taking, learning, and recall
- Show specific relationships, such as cause-effect, sequence, or comparison-contrast
- Synthesize information from different locations in the text or from multiple texts
- Convey understanding of information and concepts so misconceptions can be seen

Directions

1. Explain the purpose of using a graphic organizer to visualize how ideas link together.
2. Model how to complete a specific type of graphic organizer before asking students to complete that type in pairs and then individually.
3. After introducing several graphic organizers one at a time, present a variety of graphic organizers together so students see how the shape of each graphic organizer shows how the information is connected.
4. Model for students how to select a graphic organizer depending on the purpose for organizing information: comparison, sequence, cause-effect, main idea-supporting detail, pro/con evidence, and so on.
5. Help students select an appropriate graphic organizer.
6. Assist students as needed while they organize the information.
7. Ask students how completing the graphic organizer helped them understand the text differently. Students might discuss this using a **Think-Pair-Share** or complete a **Quick Write** to respond.

Extensions

- Have students show their graphic organizers to one another and compare their responses.
- Have students design creative variations of graphic organizers to match the content or context.
- Have students use their completed graphic organizers as study guides, outlines for essays or other writing, or cue charts for question generating/answering a text; for example: What is the main idea? What were the turning points in the chapter? What are the important steps in this process?

Analytic Graphic Organizers for Vocabulary Development

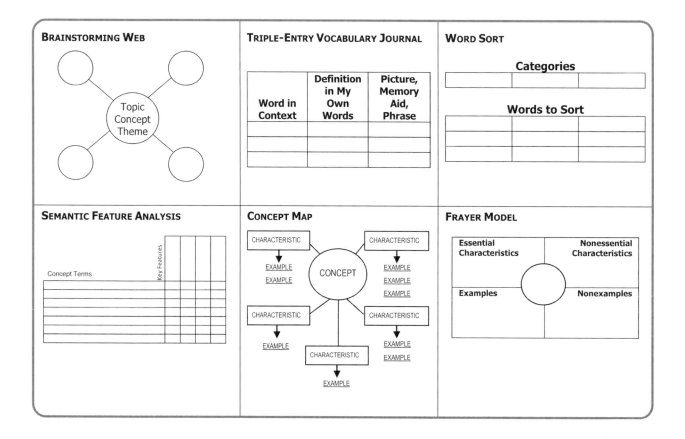

Analytic Graphic Organizers for Patterns and Relationships

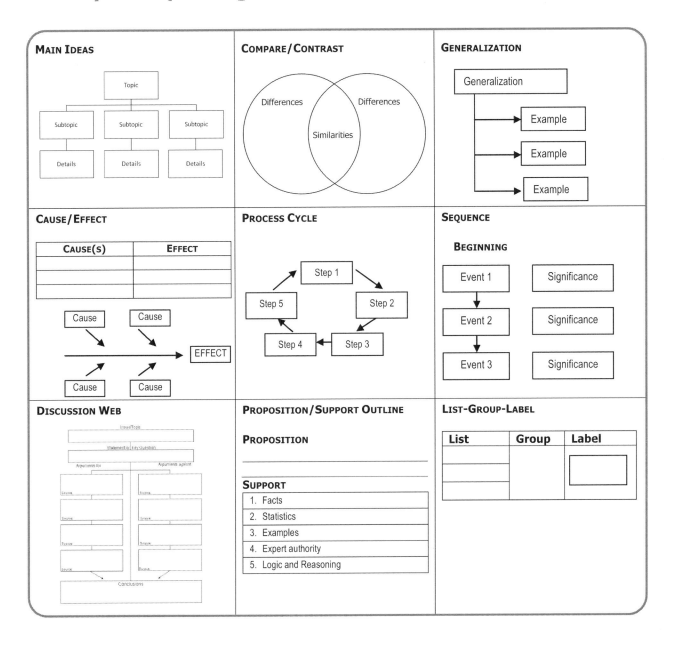

Analytic Graphic Organizers Content Examples

Mathematics

Elementary School

While reading and solving release items from the state mathematics assessment test, have students define math vocabulary words in a **Triple-Entry Vocabulary Journal**.

Word in Context	Your Definition	Your Memory Aid
What is the range of the data for these six months?	The difference between the largest number and smallest number.	13, 20, 31, 46, 59, 68 $68 - 13 = 55$
What is the perimeter, in centimeters, of the triangle?	The length around the triangle.	3 10 9 $3 + 10 + 9 = 22$ cm
Which angle appears to be obtuse?	An angle between 90° and 180°	

Middle School

Step 1
Step 5
Step 2
Step 4
Step 3

Help students remember the correct order in which to perform the mathematical operations in an expression by having them make a step process cycle. Have students enter the visual organizer in their math reference journal as another way to remember order of operations.

For example, fill in the Process Cycle with the following: *Step 1* operation inside grouping symbols first; *Step 2* exponents next; *Step 3* then multiplication and division in order from left to right; *Step 4* and finally addition and subtraction in order from left to right.

High School

While reading the review section on classification of real and rational numbers, have students use a Venn diagram as a visual organizer of the classification of these numbers.

For example, fill in the Venn diagram with the following: write the terms, real and rational numbers, in the *Similarities* section. Write in the left side *Differences* the following terms: integers, whole numbers, natural numbers, odd numbers, and even numbers. Write on the right side of *Differences* the following terms: non-integral numbers, terminating decimals, repeating decimals.

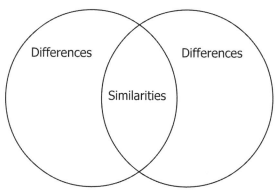

Differences   Differences

Similarities

Science

Elementary School

Help students understand how to support main ideas with evidence by having them create a main idea graphic during reading. Initially, give them the main ideas and gradually let them find the main ideas on their own.

Example of student work for the science chapter on the desert.

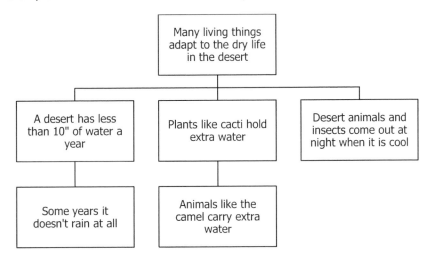

Middle School

In an earth science class, do a discovery lab where students look at different minerals while completing a classification graphic organizer of the different characteristics of each.

	Talc	Gypsum	Calcite	Fluorite	Feldspar	Quartz	Topaz
Color							
Luster							
Streak							
Hardness							
Cleavage & Fracture							
Special Properties							

High School

Have students analyze the graphic organization of the Periodic Table of the Elements to answer questions about why the different elements are placed where they are, and what the colors, Roman numerals, and numbers mean. Then have them review the website http://www.visual-literacy.org/pages/documents.htm to see many other ways of graphically organizing information.

Social Studies

Elementary School

During a geography unit on the historical Native Americans of the Southwest, have students take notes as they read using a classification graphic organizer.

Native American Group	Land and Climate	Food and Agriculture	Language and Customs	Houses
Hopi	NE Arizona Warm, dry	Raise sheep Vegetable farms	Hopi language Rain dances with snakes	Adobe and stone houses, like apartments
Navajo	NW New Mexico, Arizona, SE Utah Warm, dry	Raise sheep, cattle, and goats Hunt and gather food	Like Apache language Cured sickness with sand painting	Earth and log houses called Hogans
Pueblo	N Arizona, W New Mexico Warm, dry	Farming – corn and cotton Hunting	3 languages: Keresan, Tewa, Zuni. Dance to get good crops	Mud and stone houses called pueblos

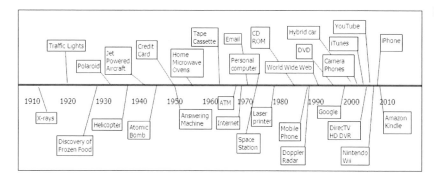

Middle School

To help students understand how much the USA has changed in a short time, have students create a timeline of change from 1900–2010. Let students pick a topic such as technology, civil rights, animal populations, immigration, or wars.

High School

In a review of the federal system in an American History class, have the students use their choice of a Venn diagram or a **Concept Map** to summarize the key aspects of the division of power between the national government and the states.

Power delegated to national government
- Armed forces
- Copyright and patent laws
- Foreign trade and policy
- Federal courts
- Interstate trade

Shared powers
- Taxes and borrowing
- Public welfare
- Criminal justice
- Banks

Powers reserved for states
- Local governments
- Schools
- Corporation laws
- Elections
- Public safety
- Marriage and divorce laws
- Trade in the state

English Language Arts

Elementary School

Use an **Analytic Graphic Organizer** to illustrate the different steps in the writing process.

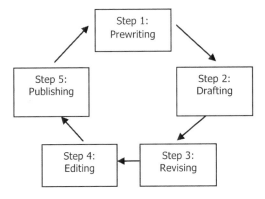

Middle School

During learning about analyzing literature, use an **Analytic Graphic Organizer** to help students make assertions and support them with paraphrased evidence from the text. Example: Lowry, L. (1993) *The Giver*. New York: Bantam Books.

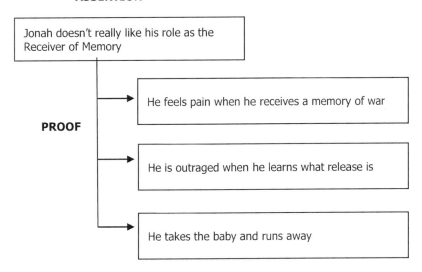

High School

During a study of authors and their work, use an **Analytic Graphic Organizer** to help students think about biographical events authors experience and how those events are reflected in their writing.

Ernest Hemingway

EVENT	SIGNIFICANCE IN WRITING
Became an expatriate in Paris when he was in his twenties	This experience influenced *The Sun Also Rises*
Started off as a reporter and journalist	This may have influenced his writing style, which has been characterized as economical
He was injured on a trip to Africa	This shows up in *The Snows of Kilimanjaro*

Semantic Feature Analysis

Description

This analytical strategy helps students examine related concepts by recording distinctions between terms according to particular criteria across which the concepts can be compared (Anders and Bos, 1986).

Purpose

Use *before*, *during*, and *after* reading to

- Build vocabulary by developing a conceptual understanding of key vocabulary terms
- Develop a visual representation of the elements or characteristics of key concepts
- Develop the analytical skills of categorizing and comparing/contrasting
- Activate prior knowledge when used *before* reading
- Assess student understanding when used *during* or *after* reading

Directions

1. Select a reading that discusses many examples of a single concept, such as a chapter in a content-area textbook or a short story with many characters.

2. Select a category of concepts to be analyzed.

   Examples: types of government, mammals, geometric shapes, human diseases, characters in a play, ecosystems

3. Using the **Semantic Feature Analysis** template, list several terms within this concept down the left vertical column. Across the top, list several key features (traits, properties, criteria, or characteristics) associated with any of the examples listed down the left side.

4. Model the process of completing the grid using a **Think-Aloud** to explain your thinking to the students as you determine whether to mark a term with a **+**, **-**, or **?**.

5. Have students read the text selection and then code, based on their reading, what key features are associated with which terms. This can be done individually or in pairs. Students should enter a plus sign (**+**) if the term typically possesses that feature, a minus sign (**−**) if the term does not typically include that feature, and a question mark (**?**) if, according to the reading, it is debatable or depends upon the specific context/situation whether the feature is applicable.

6. Compare individual or paired responses in small groups. Examine the grid and discuss similarities and differences between the concept terms. If two terms have the same patterns, discuss if there is a feature that differentiates them that could be added to the list.

Extensions

- Have students develop generalizations that can be tested against the grid.
- Divide the key feature columns into *before* and *after* so students can see how their thinking changes when the **Semantic Feature Analysis** is done before and after reading.
- Challenge students to come up with different examples and additional key features.
- Have students create the concept terms and features on their own, based on the reading.

Semantic Feature Analysis Template

Name _____   Date _____

Reading selection _____

Topic _____

Directions

After you read the text selection, code what characteristics are associated with which terms.
Codes:

+	If the term typically possesses that feature
−	If the term does not typically include that characteristic
?	If it is debatable or if the key feature depends upon the specific context/situation

Concept Terms	Key Features						

Semantic Feature Analysis Content Examples

English Language Arts

After reading narrative, epic, humorous, dramatic, ballad, free verse, and lyric forms of poetry

Help students understand the different literary devices used in different forms of poetry.

	N	E	H	D	B	F	L
Stanzas							
Meter pattern							
Rhyme scheme							
Word repetition							
Accented syllables							
Refrain							
Alliteration							

Mathematics

During reading of trigonometry text chapter on triangles

Use Semantic Feature Analysis to help students understand how various triangles are used in trigonometry to problem-solve real situations.

	Equi-angular	Acute	Obtuse	Right
Distance between various points in the universe				
Projective force and velocity				
Electric circuits				
Architectural design				
Light refraction				

Science

Before, during, and *after* reading about systems of the body

Help students determine the interrelationships (or not) of human systems that impact health.
Systems codes:
S = Skeletal M = Muscular E = Endocrine
C = Cardiovascular D = Digestive U = Urinary
L = Lymphatic R = Respiratory N= Nervous

	S	M	E	C	D	U	L	R	N
Fitness									
Heart									
Cancer									
Diabetes									
Obesity									
Liver									
Alzheimer's									

Social Studies

Before, during, and *after* reading about economic systems in various countries and their impacts on the average citizen

Use Semantic Feature Analysis to predict and confirm the impact of elements of economic systems in various countries upon its people.

	US	Can	Mex	GB	Jap	Chi	Iraq
Employment							
Healthcare							
Retirement							
Recreation							
Education							
Agriculture							
Cultural arts							

Discussion Web (Social Studies)

Description

This **Analytic Graphic Organizer**, which works particularly well with social studies/history content, promotes critical thinking by encouraging students to take a position for or against a particular point of view. The strategy requires students to establish and support evidence for their selected point of view based on their reading of narrative or expository texts (Duthie, 1986).

Purpose

Use *during* or *after* reading one or more texts to
- Provide a framework for analyzing an issue by citing evidence for or against a point of view before coming to a personal viewpoint
- Develop students' ability to draw conclusions based upon evidence, not opinion
- Provide opportunities for active discussion and collaboration
- Help students organize ideas for writing and use evidence to support their points of view
- Encourage the use of multiple resources to determine a conclusion
- Help students refine their thinking by listening to opposing information or ideas

Directions

1. Choose, or have students choose, an issue with opposing viewpoints.
2. Locate, or have students locate, a variety of resources that describe the issue.
3. Provide, or have students create, a guiding question to focus the discussion.
4. Have students work alone or in pairs to complete both sides of the discussion web, note text title and page numbers where they found the evidence, and form a tentative conclusion. Encourage them to be open-minded and suspend their personal judgment during data collection.
5. Have two pairs work together to review their discussion webs and add additional arguments. Have the four students discuss all the evidence and come to consensus about the strongest point of view, based on the evidence (not personal opinion).
6. Have students create a conclusion that summarizes the group's thinking and write it at the bottom of the web. Encourage them to avoid biased language.
7. Have each small group report their conclusions to the whole class. They should mention any dissenting viewpoints within their group. Limit the report to three minutes so all groups have time to present.
8. Have each student review his/her own tentative conclusion about the guiding question and then complete a one paragraph **Quick Write** that states the conclusion, citing the three to five key facts or reasons that support the conclusion.

Extensions

- Have students write a personal reflection about how the issue has impacted their lives or the lives of others they know.
- Have students write a response supporting the opposite point of view.
- Have students do a formal debate or "town meeting" discussion. If possible, present to an authentic audience and solicit feedback.

Discussion Web Template

Name _____   Date _____

Issue/Topic

Statement or Key Question

Arguments for   Arguments against

Source:

Source:

Source:

Source:

Source:

Source:

Source:

Source:

Conclusions

Discussion Web Content Examples

Social Studies

Elementary School

Before reading about issues in the local community, have students brainstorm topics they have heard about recently and ask them to pick a point of view on one of the issues. Then utilize the **Discussion Web** Template as a way to scaffold students in their efforts to support their opinions with evidence from their reading.

Middle School

Before reading opinions on the tension between rights and responsibilities of U.S. citizens, introduce several issues that address this notion and have students work in pairs to develop opposing viewpoints on their chosen issues using the texts provided by the instructor.

High School

Before reading about Supreme Court cases that deal with the concept of legitimate power, introduce the overviews and have groups of students choose one of the cases and develop two opposing arguments they will use to debate the issue for another class.

Proposition/Support Outline (Science)

Description

This **Analytic Graphic Organizer** asks students to set forth a hypothesis/proposition and list the arguments and evidence from the text to support or refute the statement. It is particularly effective when used with science content.

Purpose

Use *before*, *during*, and *after* reading to

- Develop higher order critical thinking skills, particularly analysis and evaluation
- Help students focus during reading as they look for supporting arguments and draw conclusions
- Help students separate fact and opinion in a reading selection and analyze the justification given to support conclusions or generalizations
- Help students identify information that reflects opinion, bias, personal viewpoints, hypotheses, and debatable assumptions or assertions

Directions

1. Introduce the term *proposition* as a statement that can be argued as true.
2. Discuss fact and opinion. Brainstorm examples and have students offer criteria for separating fact and opinion.
3. Test the student criteria using the list of proposition statements for students to identify as fact or opinion.
4. Assign a reading selection that features one or more strong propositions and have small groups of students identify the key propositions of the selection.
5. Have student groups then evaluate each of these statements, looking for evidence of opinion, bias, or personal viewpoints.
6. Have student groups identify the statement as fact or opinion after taking notes that describe the supporting evidence: facts, statistics, examples, expert authority, logic, and reasoning. (These can be put on a graphic organizer chart.)
7. Have the groups share their conclusions with the entire class. Encourage further discussion of any statement about which the groups cannot agree.

Extensions

- Use the **Proposition/Support Outline** for independent research so students scrutinize reference materials for relevant information and arguments.
- Have students write a position paper or analyze multimedia information related to a proposition, supporting it with appropriate facts, statistics, examples, expert authority, and logic/reasoning.

Proposition/Support Outline Template

Name _____   Date _____

Topic _____

Proposition _____

_____

1. Facts/Statistics	Source

2. Examples	Source

3. Expert Authority	Source

4. Conclusions (based on logical reasoning, not just preference/opinion)

This template is based on Buehl, D. (2009).

Proposition/Support Outline Content Examples

Science

Elementary School

Use the **Proposition/Support Outline** during a unit on environmental change to help students sift through the competing opinions on the impact of humans on the environment. As a class, use the *gradual release model* to teach students how to use the strategy. Put students in pairs and provide each pair with a different reading on an issue the class is studying. Have them work in pairs to complete the outlines and then discuss their findings with other groups of students. Collect the opinions of the different articles and debate those positions.

Middle School

Use the **Proposition/Support Outline** to engage students in a consideration of different points of view on any controversial topic, such as whether the United States should eliminate its use of fossil fuels. Have students work in groups or individually to complete outlines on different readings around the same topic. Use Two-Column Notes to have students keep track of each article and the strength of the proposition in each. Then use this information to have students write a short essay on the position, determining their own position and using the information from each of the articles as support.

High School

Have students use **Proposition/Support Outlines** to analyze information from multi-media sources as well as traditional text on an issue under investigation by the class, such as the use of stem cells in medical research. Have students search for three different high quality web-based sources of information, using the outlines to determine the extent to which each source effectively supports its position. Then, have students work in two groups to identify the different points of view represented on the topic and stage a debate between the two different positions.

Inference Notes Wheel (English Language Arts)

Description

This **Analytic Graphic Organizer** is particularly useful in the English language arts classroom. The organizer asks students to record literal (in the text) information about a topic or person in the inside wedges and inferential interpretations in the outer wedges of a circle to help students draw tentative conclusions from cues in text (adapted from Burke, 2002).

Purpose

Use *during* and *after* reading to

- Draw tentative conclusions about what is not directly stated or observable
- Understand literal statements may contain inferential clues that require interpretation by the reader
- Understand that evidence-based inferences and conclusions result from information in the text that can be cited and may not be derived solely from personal opinion or knowledge

Directions

1. Prior to the lesson, identify a reading selection that requires inferential thinking in several cases to develop full understanding of what the text is saying about a topic or person.

2. Select six quotes from the selection that relate to a specific topic or person and place them in the inner wedges of the inference notes wheel. Complete one or two of the inferential responses to model what an inferential response contains.

3. Begin instruction by discussing how inferences are derived from literal information, using real life examples. Explain that since an inference is partially based on evidence and partially upon personal experience, an inference is possible or probable, but not certain.
   Examples
   - It is cloudy outside. What might happen? (snow, rain, or stay cloudy)
   - The man was frowning and his arms were crossed. What might he be feeling? (anger, frustration, confusion, shyness, or discomfort)

4. Brainstorm context cues or patterns students can use to know when inferential thinking is required.
   Examples
   - Adjectives or adverbs provide a clue about emotions or possible action
   - A list or several pieces of information close in the text lead to a generalization
   - A description of a setting can be used to create a mood
   - A metaphor/symbol can be used to describe a person's character or probable action

5. Have students work in pairs or small groups to discuss and complete the rest of the inference notes wheel for the passage.

6. When the inference notes wheel is complete, have the students write a summary conclusion about the topic or person and support their analysis with quotes and citations from the text.

7. Continue to have students use the inference notes wheel with other text passages and gradually have the students select the literal information on their own.

Extensions

- Before reading, have students preview reading selections to select the subject they will take inference notes about during reading.
- After reading, have students list inferences they derived from text, insert them in the outer wedges of the inference note wheel, and add supporting quotes that support the conclusion.

Inference Notes Wheel Template

Name _____ Date _____

Directions: Find six statements, examples, or quotations in the text that directly relate to the topic or character listed in the center of the wheel (or use one chosen by the teacher). Selected quotations or statements should suggest to the reader an inference beyond the literal statement in the text. Place one statement in each of the inner circle wedges and note the page number where each is found. In the outer wedge, explain your interpretation about each statement based on the cues in the text and your own knowledge about people or about the topic.

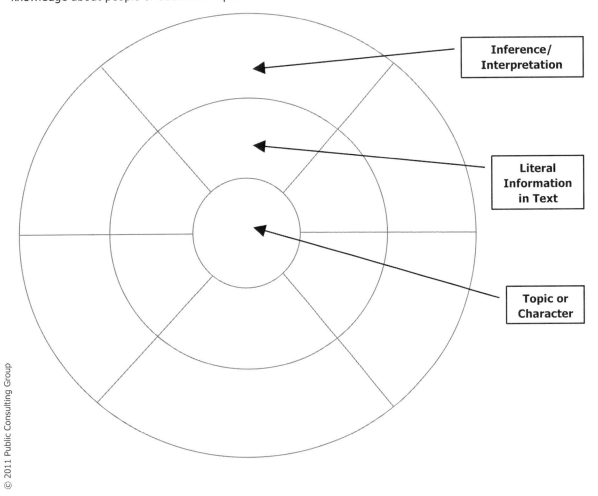

Inference/
Interpretation

Literal
Information
in Text

Topic or
Character

Conclusion: On the back of this sheet, summarize the inferences you made about the topic or character, based on the six inferential statements, and explain how your analysis was based on the evidence in the text. Use direct quotations or citation information to support your reasoning.

Inference Notes Wheel Content Example

English Language Arts

Elementary School

While reading *Bud, Not Buddy*, by Christopher Paul Curtis, use the **Inference Notes Wheel** to help students develop an understanding of inference and how to think about indirect presentation of character traits.

Character: Bud

Quote: "We were all standing in line for breakfast when one of the caseworkers came in and tap-tap-tapped down the line."

Inference: The narrator is living in an orphanage

Middle School

During and *after* reading *Autumn Street*, by Lois Lowry, have students use the **Inference Notes Wheel** to build their ability to support their ideas. Work with them to develop propositions about the text. Have them place these in the outer circle. Then, have them identify quotes that support those propositions in the middle circle.

Topic: The effect of WWII on families in the U.S.

Quote: "Pearl Harbor is on the radio, Daddy," I told him, "And Mama is crying." After that, the answer to everything was "Because of the War." After that, there were air raid drills at kindergarten. We had to run, holding hands, to the subway station and hide there. Because of the war.

Inference: Pearl Harbor led to a great deal of fear in America

High School

During the study of complex texts, use **Inference Notes Wheels** to examine different aspects of a text. Use these as prewriting for a longer essay or paper about the novel. For example, while studying F. S. Fitzgerald's *The Great Gatsby*, complete inference notes wheels either on several different characters or on several aspects of one of the main characters. Use each wheel as the basis for one section of a longer paper.

Character: Jay Gatsby's Motivation

Quote: "That huge place there?" she cried pointing. "Do you like it?" "I love it, but I don't see how you live there all alone." "I keep it always full of interesting people, night and day. People who do interesting things. Celebrated people."

Inference: Gatsby's Tragic Flaw

Five-Step Problem Solving Organizer (Mathematics)

Description

This **Analytic Graphic Organizer** provides a step-by-step reasoning process for students can use to set up and solve mathematical word problems (Braselton & Decker, 1994).

The diamond shape of the arrows reinforces that

- a word problem (top point of the diamond)
- can be solved in multiple ways (middle of the diamond)
- but results in the same convergent conclusion (bottom point of the diamond).

Purpose

Use *during* and *after* reading to

- Improve students' abilities to read and solve math word problems
- Activate prior knowledge and experience that can be used to solve new problems
- Provide a graphic structure that helps students use a step-by-step problem-solving technique and remember that a single math problem with a single conclusion may be solved in multiple ways

Directions

Show students the diamond-shaped graphic organizer as you introduce the five-step problem solving process.

1. Explain that the top point of the diamond is the precise problem statement and the bottom point of the diamond is the precise answer.

2. Explain that the process occurring in the middle section of the diamond can involve a variety of problem solving steps that depend on prior knowledge and reasoning about the problem, but will lead to the same solution.

3. Explain **Step 1**, *understanding and restating the problem*. Encourage students to ask themselves the following questions:
   - What are you trying to find out or solve?
   - Do you understand all of the vocabulary in the problem?
   - What information is known?
   - What information is unknown or unneeded?
   - How can you restate the problem in your own words so it is clear and makes sense?

4. Discuss **Step 2**, *how to find needed data/information*. Prompt students to consider:
   - What key words are provided that suggest the type of operation that needs to be performed?
   - What formulas or equations are suggested from the numerical data?

Directions (continued)

5. Discuss the types of strategies that can be used in **Step 3**, *plan how to solve the problem*. These might include:

    o   creating a chart, diagram, picture, or model;

    o   writing an equation or using a formula;

    o   determining if there are patterns;

    o   guess and check;

    o   or working backwards.

6. Discuss **Step 4**, *finding the answer*. Perform and keep any calculations or other actions needed and check each step of the plan as it is accomplished.

7. Confirm that, in **Step 5**, the answer is reviewed against the original problem to check if the answer makes sense and is reasonable. Emphasize that this is the most important step in the five-step process.

8. Illustrate the process by modeling the thinking involved in each step using a simple, actual problem.

9. Have small groups solve several problems using the organizer, discussing their thinking for each step.

10. Remind students that **Five-Step Problem Solving** is a guide to problem solving, but it does not provide a set formula for calculating or solving problems.

Extensions

After students use the five-step process to solve a problem, determine if the techniques would work for other problems or if there were multiple techniques used by students for finding the solution.

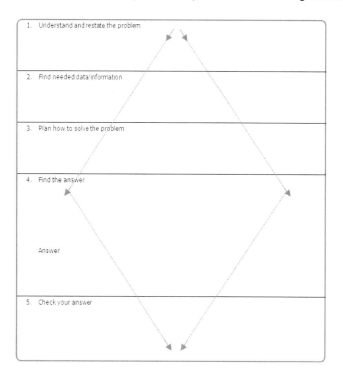

Five-Step Problem Solving Template

Name _____   Date _____

Directions: Use this organizer when working on a word problem. First, decide what you are trying to find out or solve. Then, list the data/information you need to solve the problem. The next steps are to describe your plan for solving the problem, derive the answer, and then check it against the original problem to be sure your answer makes sense and double-check that the solution is correct.

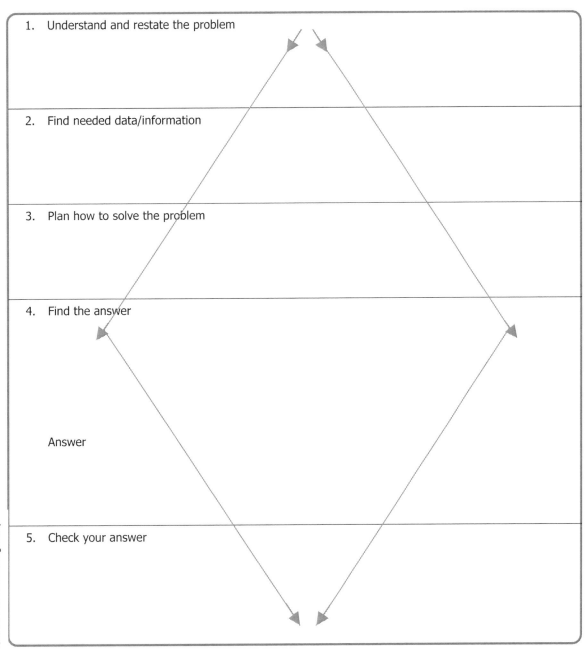

1. Understand and restate the problem

2. Find needed data/information

3. Plan how to solve the problem

4. Find the answer

   Answer

5. Check your answer

Five-Step Problem Solving Organizer Example

Mathematics

Elementary School

To improve students' ability to solve math word problems using fractions and percents, present them with a **Five-Step Problem Solving Organizer**.

- Re-state the problem.

- Molly sings in the chorus at her school. In the chorus, 3/5 of the students are in the sixth grade, and the rest are in the fifth grade. What fraction in the chorus are fifth graders? Write your answer from part (a) as a percent.

- What are you trying to solve? How many students in the chorus are fifth graders?

- Find needed data. 3/5 of the chorus is sixth graders. The chorus is made up of fifth and sixth graders.

- Write an equation. $3/5 +$ ___ $= 1$ answer 2/5 $2 \div 5 = 10$

Middle School

The **Five-Step Problem Solving Organizer** can be used to guide students to identify multiple approaches to solving single mathematical problem. Ask students to explain two different ways to derive the answer when completing Step 4. Here are two examples of solutions for the following problem.

Problem

Henry is making a model plane. The plan is approximately 200 inches long and 50 inches tall. He wants the model to be 10 inches long. How tall should the model be? Show or explain how you found your answer.

— = —; $200x = 500$; $x = 2.5$

Or

The plan is – as tall as it is long. So the model should be – × 10 or 2.5 inches tall.

High School

Solving SAT mathematics questions requires students to activate prior knowledge from more than one skill, concept, or mathematics content standard. To help high school students unpack these problems, give them the **Five-Step Problem Solving Organizer** as they work through the SAT prep book. Remind them to pay close attention to what the problem is asking and what key words help them determine how to solve the problem. Also remind them to consider if the problem can be worked backwards or if there are possible options that can be eliminated.

Think-Pair-Share

Description

This is a cooperative discussion strategy that emphasizes what students should do at each of the three steps of the protocol: think, pair, and share (Lyman, 1981).

Purpose

Use *before*, *during*, or *after* reading to

- Allow for reflection and sharing before whole group discussion
- Provide time for everyone to formulate responses to the reading, experience, or prompt

Directions

1. Create a question, prompt, or problem to generate student thinking.

2. Have students spend two to three minutes brainstorming or thinking individually about the question asked or problem posed. Option: Have students do a **Quick Write** of their thoughts.

3. Have students share their ideas with a partner for two to three minutes.

4. Have students share their most significant ideas with the whole group, taking care to not repeat what someone else has already reported.

Extensions

- Stop at a planned point during an interactive read aloud and have students **Think-Pair-Share** about a possible solution to the character's problem; a prediction about what might happen next, or supporting detail about a content concept.

- Schedule **Think-Pair-Shares** during silent reading to stimulate thinking and interaction with text.

- Use **Think-Pair-Share** as a strategy to enhance active listening during lectures, presentations, or demonstrations.

Think-Pair-Share Template

Name _____   Date _____

Directions

Write the question or problem in the space below.

Think
Write three answers or ideas you have about this question or problem.
1.

2.

3.

Pair
Discuss your ideas with a partner. Check any ideas above that your partner also wrote down. Write down ideas your partner had that you did not.

1.

2.

3.

Share
Review all of your ideas and circle the one you think is most important. One of you will share this idea with the whole group. As you listen to the ideas of others, write down three you liked.

1.

2.

3.

Think-Pair-Share Content Example

English Language Arts

Before learning about writing for specific audiences.

Brainstorm a list of different types of books and the people who might read each type. Then introduce the Think-Pair-Share activity, using the protocol to address the following question: "How do books look and sound different when they are written for different audiences?"

Once the pairs have completed their discussion, draw two columns on the board/digital display. Ask each pair to share an important point, but to be careful not to repeat the same point shared by another group.

Write each pair's most important idea on the board in the left column. In the right column, have students suggest other similar examples.

Use this information to begin a class discussion about keeping your audience in mind when writing.

Mathematics

Before and *during* reading an introduction on probability

Pose the following question: How do you make decisions? Ask students to do a **Quick Write** of their thoughts about this and then turn and share their ideas with a partner for two to three minutes.

Ask each pair to share the similarities and differences in decision-making approaches. Record this information on chart paper and ask students to keep these in mind as they read the introduction.

After reading, have students think about how their decision-making processes might or might not be influenced by statistics. Then have students pair to discuss and then share with the class. This builds background knowledge for the forthcoming unit.

Science

Before a lesson sequence about the phases of the moon, post the following questions and have students record their ideas using the **Think Pair Share** protocol.

1. Think on your own: What do you think causes the phases of the moon? How are moon phases different from eclipses?

2. Pair with a partner to discuss

3. Share the most important ideas you discussed with the larger group

After studying the phases through direct observation, modeling and readings, have students return to this record of their initial thinking and make corrections to anything that may have been incorrect in their original explanation.

Social Studies

During a unit on leaders of the civil rights movement, use **Think Pair Share** at various points as a way to help students consolidate their learning, review material, and generate questions.

For example, divide the class into groups and assign each group one key civil rights leader. Ask the students to read the section in the book on their leader and to do some online research about the person, jotting notes as they read.

In each group, ask students to complete the **Think Pair Share** protocol in reference to their assigned leader. Have students think about the most interesting and important facts they learned about this person and then to share them with the small group. Then ask each group to share with the class.

Record the results on the board/digital display and use them as a way to discuss the differences among these leaders with students.

Reciprocal Teaching

Description

Reciprocal teaching is a **Collaborative Routine** for improving reading comprehension. Four-person teams use the skills of summarizing, questioning, clarifying, and predicting to bring meaning to the text (Palincsar & Brown, 1984).

Purpose

Use *during* reading to

- Improve students' skills at summarizing, questioning, clarifying, and predicting
- Help struggling readers practice the habits and skills of strong readers
- Encourage collaborative exploration of text

Directions

1. Create groups of four students.
2. Distribute one note card to each member of the group identifying each person's role.

   a. summarizer   c. clarifier

   b. questioner   d. predictor

3. Have students silently read a few paragraphs of the assigned text selection. Encourage them to use note taking strategies such as selective underlining or sticky notes to help them better prepare for their role in the discussion.
4. At a given stopping point, the Summarizer will highlight key ideas up to this point in the reading.
5. The Questioner will then pose questions about the selection.
6. The Clarifier addresses confusing parts and attempts to answer the questions.
7. The Predictor can offer guesses about what the author will tell the group next.
8. The roles in the group then switch one person to the right, and the next selection is read. Students repeat the process using their new roles. This continues until the entire selection is read.

It is important to teach, model, and practice each role/skill before expecting students to do all four together.

Possible Verbal Prompts

Summarizer: The important ideas in what I read are _____

Questioner: What connections can I make? How does this information change what I was thinking? What is the author telling me by this comment?

Clarifier: I do not understand the part where _____

            I need to know more about _____

Predictor: I think_____, I wonder_____, I predict_____

Extensions

- Use with **Paired Reading** or **Save the Last Word for Me**.
- Have students write individual summaries after they finish reading and discussing the selection together.

Reciprocal Teaching Template

Name _____   Date _____

Directions: Read the selection and take notes on the four comprehension strategies in preparation for the Reciprocal Teaching group activity.

Summarize

Question

Clarify

Predict

Reciprocal Teaching Content Examples

English Language Arts

During small group reading of a novel, play, short story, or other genre

Adapt literature circle roles to the four roles of Reciprocal Teaching, rotating them at appropriate pause points in the text reading and specifying areas of focus to deepen the discussion past literal interpretation; use H. Quiroga's *The Alligator War* as an example.

- *Summarizer:* Parallel the alligator behaviors to people's behaviors during the summary.

- Questioner*:* Ask only questions that require inferential thinking.

- *Clarifier:* Be the wise old alligator when you respond to the questions.

- *Predictor:* Compare human beings to alligators in predicting what will happen if a warship again goes up the river.

Mathematics

During small group completion of college entrance exam practice tests

Involve students in actively discussing the types of exam questions and techniques for answering them by applying the Reciprocal Teaching roles to the sample questions.

- *Summarizer:* State numerical math problems in words or word problems in numbers and symbols.

- *Questioner:* Ask about vocabulary or process steps to solve the problem.

- *Clarifier:* Explain vocabulary or process steps.

- *Predictor:* Predict that the detractor answer test makers include is easy to select if the problem isn't carefully thought out.

Science

During reading of a difficult chemistry chapter on chemical equilibrium and Le Chatelier's Principle

Have students take on the four roles of *Summarizer, Questioner, Clarifier,* and *Predictor* after reading each of the sections. Tell each role to focus on specific content when reading.

- *Summarizer:* Focus on the opening and closing paragraphs of each 1–2 page section

- *Questioner:* Read the Section Review Questions and ask the group any you don't understand yourself.

- *Clarifier:* Review the graphs and figures that explain the reactions.

- *Predictor*: Read the sample problems and Chemistry in Action tips to predict why it matters for students to understand chemical equilibrium.

Social Studies

Before, during, and *after* reading a chapter on problems of the presidency with the case study of Watergate

Ask small groups of students to compare the President's problems during Watergate with the problems of today's President, focusing on the theme: does the President have too many jobs and too much power?

Have students guide their discussion by taking on the four roles of Reciprocal Teaching: *Summarizer, Questioner, Clarifier,* and *Predictor.*

Paired Reading

Description

This combined reading comprehension and fluency strategy supports students to be actively involved in the structured reading aloud of a shared text. Students benefit from the intensive sessions of reading, speaking, and active listening.

Purpose

Use *during* reading to

- Give students practice in oral reading; to build fluency
- Provide practice with active listening, reading aloud, and summarizing
- Promote active engagement with reading
- Develop specific skills related to reading comprehension

Directions

1. Basic paired reading requires establishing ground rules about when and how help will be asked for/offered when reading, how turns will be taken, and what each role will include. One basic set of ground rules might be the following.
   - In pairs, take turns reading a paragraph at a time from an assigned reading.
   - The reader reads in a low voice, loud enough only for the listener to hear.
   - When the reader completes the paragraph, the listener provides a summary of the paragraph that needs to be "approved" by the reader. If the summary is not clear or accurate, the pair goes back to the text and rereads silently to add what is necessary.
   - Then the two switch roles, with the first reader becoming the active listener and summarizer.
   - If the reader stumbles on a word or is having difficulty, the reader can ask for help from the partner. If help is not asked for, then the listener should give the reader the opportunity to figure it out.

2. Give directions for what the pair should do when they finish reading. Possible options include:
   - Discussing what they each found interesting about what they have read
   - Answering questions or completing a graphic organizer together or separately
   - Interviewing another pair about their reading session (what went well/what did not)
   - Asking pairs to contribute three interesting words (or words that meet specific criteria) from their reading to the **Word Wall**.
   - Adding to their learning log or journal based on what was read
   - Asking the partners to write a collaborative summary of what they read

Extensions

- Extend the listening/summarizing role to include clarifying, predicting, and questioning.
- Let readers read longer segments of the text before switching roles.
- Give pairs a set of cards that direct them to do different things with the text: visualize, clarify, make a connection, etc. The listener picks a card before the reader begins to read and then shares according to the card after the reader completes the section.

Paired Reading Content Examples

English Language Arts	Mathematics
After viewing the video and *during* the reading of Shakespeare's *As You Like It*	*During* reading of review information about algebraic expressions prior to the unit on functions and graphs
Model for students how to do a Paired Read using Jaques' speech, *The Seven Ages of Man*. Show students how they are to summarize the plot actions and the ways character actions and dialogue show how the character feels about life.	Use Paired Reads to have students read and summarize the text pages on addition, subtraction, multiplication, and division of algebraic expressions. Tell students to focus their summaries on defining the related math terms, and recognizing an example when mathematically represented in numbers and symbols.
Then have students do Paired Reads intermittently throughout the reading of the play to help students comprehend difficult sections.	
Science	**Social Studies**
During a reading about Newton's Second Law of Motion	*Before, during,* and *after* reading about Roosevelt's New Deal
After a lesson sequence about the Second Law of Motion, have students do a Paired Read to summarize a text explanation of Newton's Second Law with the key outcome of understanding.	Have pairs of students read about the New Deal in a variety of texts or online resources. Stress that during their summary responses, students should focus on learning how the New Deal would impact American life in relation to
• The inversely proportional relationship of acceleration and mass • The predicted results when acceleration, net force, or mass changes	• Labor and employment • Housing • Business and the economy • Farm programs and rural life • Retirement

Critical Thinking Cue Questions

Description

Questions related to the six thinking skills in Bloom's Taxonomy are purposely constructed to ensure students are stimulated to respond at all levels of the cognitive domain, especially the higher levels. Students may be asked to respond through **Quick Writes**, learning logs, tests, creative writing that answers the six prompts, **Role-Audience-Format-Topic (RAFT)** activities, or other writing or speaking activities.

Purpose

Use *before*, *during*, and *after* reading to:

- Establish a purpose for reading
- Help students develop their thinking skills at all levels of cognition
- Ensure learning assignments respond to all levels of cognition
- Deepen student comprehension of text, especially at the higher levels
- Stimulate original thinking through the use of open-ended questions
- Provide an array of questions to support students to demonstrate what they have learned

Directions

1. Assess the cognitive demands of the reading assignment to determine which of the six levels of thinking are required for students to understand what they are reading.
2. Explicitly teach the students about Critical Thinking Cue Questions and share a copy of the cue questions with them.
3. Develop questions in advance about the text and give them to students before they read, to provide a purpose for engaging with the text.
4. Model how to respond to Bloom's thinking levels through **Think-Alouds**, whole group discussions, small group discussions, paired answers, and other methods to learn how to answer questions at the six levels.
5. Once students are comfortable with the six levels of thinking skills, assign independent after-reading tasks using questions from the chart.

Extensions

- Provide choice for student responses by offering several questions from which they select one to answer for each of the six levels.
- Have students use the chart when previewing text before they read to set their own purposes for reading.
- Ask students to construct questions and answers about what they have read, using the cue questions on the chart.

Note: While these cues typically apply where shown on the display, the context of the complete question or passage may change the cognitive demand in some cases.

Critical Thinking Cue Questions

Based on Bloom's Taxonomy

Lower-Order Thinking Skills	Higher-Order Thinking Skills	
1. REMEMBER	**4. ANALYZE**	• Makes
• Called	• Allow, not allow, criteria	• Needs
• Describe	• Analyze, assess	• Next, next step
• How many	• But, except, exception	• Observe
• Identify	• Cause	• Pattern
• Is, are	• Check	• Predict, hypothesize
• Label	• Classify, organize	• Prevent, precaution
• List	• Compare, contrast	• Priority
• Memorize	• Conclude, conclusion	• Problem, situation
• Name	• Correct, proper, incorrect	• Process
• Recall	• Determine, diagnose,	• Purpose, motive
• Recognize	suspect	• Question
• Repeat	• Difference, differs	• Relate, relationship
• Select	• Distinguish, differentiate	• Representation
• State	• Divide, break apart	• Review
• What, what is/are/does	• Evidence	• Separate, divide, pull apart
• When	• Examine	• Sequence, order
• Where	• Failure	• Solve, troubleshoot
• Which	• Idea, concept	• Symbol
• Who	• Identify, indicate	• Symptom, complaint, sign
• Fill-in-the-missing-word sentences	• If, if - then	• Test
	• Infer	• Than, rather than
	• Like, unlike	• Theme
	• Logical	• True/false
2. UNDERSTAND	**5. EVALUATE**	• Importance
• Define	• Advantages	• Judge
• Discuss	• Affect	• Justify
• Example	• Agree	• Opinion
• Explain	• Appraise	• Optimum
• How	• Appropriate	• Perception, perspective
• Locate	• Assess	• Prioritize
• Mean	• Better, best (-er, -est	• Probable
• Paraphrase	words)	• Prove, disprove
• Restate	• Choose	• Rate, rank
• Summarize	• Consider	• Recommend, suggest
• Translate	• Criticize	• Support
• Visualize	• Defend	• Value, quality
	• Disagree	• What could this mean
	• Evaluate	

Lower-Order Thinking Skills		Higher-Order Thinking Skills	
3. APPLY	• Give example	**6. CREATE**	• Maximize
• Action	• Illustrate	• Adapt	• Minimize
• Apply	• Operate	• Alternative	• Modify
• Assemble	• Perform	• Change, substitute	• Predict
• Build a model	• Plan, prepare	• Could	• Propose alternative
• Calculate	• Procedure	• Create	• Put it all together
• Construct	• Proper, acceptable	• Elaborate	• Synthesize
• Demonstrate	• Schedule	• Formulate	• Theorize
• Do, be done	• Show	• Imagine	• What could be
• Dramatize	• Sketch	• Improve	• What if
• Draw	• Solve	• Invent	
• Duplicate, reproduce	• Use, employ		
• Function	• Visualize		
	• Write		

Based on Cochran & Conklin (2007).

Critical Thinking Questions Content Examples

English Language Arts	Mathematics
During and *after* reading a classic novel with complex plot, characterization, and theme	*Before and after* reading a text chapter on measurement
During reading, provide cue questions for students to respond at all cognitive levels: knowledge, comprehension, application, analysis, evaluation, synthesis.	*Before* reading, students activate prior knowledge and predict what will be learned by answering six one-minute **Quick Write** prompts that relate to precision, accuracy, and units of measurement. Each question is based on one of the six levels of Bloom's Critical Thinking Taxonomy.
After *reading*, provide a chart of cue questions for each of the six types of critical thinking levels and have students create and answer questions to communicate their learning.	*After* reading, review and revise the predictive responses to demonstrate understanding of how precision, accuracy, and measurement units affect mathematical predictions and estimates.
Science	**Social Studies**
During reading of a text chapter, reviewing graphic depictions, and viewing a video on plate tectonics	*Before, during,* and, *after* reading editorials about the economic systems in several countries
Structure a **Two-Column Note Taking** chart with prompts that require students to analyze, evaluate, and synthesize information on plate tectonics and correlate it with geological features in today's world.	Have students write a persuasive essay about the country they think has the most effective economic system and justify the response by analytical comparisons, evaluative judgments about quality, and a synthesizing description about how other countries would benefit from adopting the economic system.

Use of *Analytic Graphic Organizer* and *Interactive Word Wall* in a Middle School Mathematics Classroom

Ms. Bouchard hands out a list of mathematical terms and a **Five-Step Problem-Solving Analytic Graphic Organizer** to her third block pre-Algebra students. Most students barely look up as she walks around the groups of desks and lays the sheets on each—they are too busy reviewing and discussing the board work. Sounds unlikely? That's what Ms. Bouchard thought before she tried the strategy. But the students know that on Mondays and Fridays there will be a word problem related to real life dilemmas and a flawed solution that needs to be corrected. And they come in ready to work.

Before Reading/Learning

Today's problem begins with someone spilling Pepsi onto a keyboard and concerns whether the owner of the laptop made a mistake by not buying an extended warranty. The problem requires careful reading about depreciation, replacement costs, interest rates, and warranty details and combines application of math knowledge, higher order thinking, and critical reading of mathematically dense text—all lifelong mathematical literacy habits Ms. Bouchard wants her students to develop.

Ms. Bouchard rings a chime to indicate that each group has five minutes to complete their response, including a mathematical presentation and rationale statement for why the solution presented in the problem is flawed. She rings the chime again in five minutes. She picks a number from a hat—this means student #2 in each group will be doing the presentations today. Students do not know in advance who will be chosen, so all need to be prepared.

As a member of each of the six groups presents their group's response, the others rate the mini-presentation using a short rubric that will be handed back to the presenters. Ms. Bouchard notes the presentations are much clearer, more mathematically specific, more concise, and more to the point than earlier in the year and she commends the students. Then she asks them to look at the list of terms and the Analytic Graphic Organizer she handed out at the beginning of class.

During Reading/Learning

Ms. Bouchard projects the Analytic Graphic Organizer on the Smartboard and asks students to look at the terms on the **Word Wall** and the terms on their handout. "We are going to continue with the problem solving unit by beginning with word problems that describe one variable in relation to another. These are just like the equations you were working on earlier in the week. I am going to show you how I want you to use the problem-solving analytic graphic organizer to set up and solve the word problems you will be doing. Eyes up here, please. As I talk, listen for the vocabulary terms on the sheet as well as terms that are on the Word Wall. Every time you hear me say a term that's on the sheet, check it off. If it's on the Word Wall, write it down." Several students nod; others swivel in their chairs to better see the words on the Word Wall.

Ms. Bouchard uses the words *equation, variable, unknown,* and other words on Word Wall and the handout as she explains how to use the analytic graphic organizer to solve the first problem: Anna is twice as old as Tia. Their combined age is 24 years. How old is each girl?

After she finishes explaining, Ms. Bouchard asks the students to compare with a partner the terms they heard and try to define the terms in their own words. Then she asks students to share the terms they do not know. She asks other students to provide answers or, when no one is sure, she provides a definition and example. "Okay, so are there some terms from the list we need to add to the Word Wall?" Marcus replies, "*Unknown* should be added because it means something else most of the time but has a specific meaning when you do math problems." Ellie agrees and says, "We should add *variable* for the same reason." Ms. Bouchard makes the additions. "Anything else?" The class seems satisfied with the terms chosen to support their work in this unit and students add the two terms to their **Triple-Entry Vocabulary Journals** where they note the word in context, a definition in their own words, and a strategy for remembering what the term means. Ms. Bouchard asks the students having trouble coming up with a memory strategy to consult with others in their group for ideas.

Ms. Bouchard then returns to the problem-solving analytic graphic organizer and models how to do another problem: Two CDs cost $26 dollars. One CD costs $4 more than the other does. How much did each CD cost? She directs students' attention to how to set up the problem and how to use the analytic graphic organizer to guide their thinking. After modeling a third problem, which she asks the students to do with her and complete so they have an example to guide their work, Ms. Bouchard asks them to work in pairs through three more problems in the math textbook using the organizer. She points to a thick stack of blank analytic graphic organizers on her desk and asks that one person in each pair get three organizers.

Students quickly get to work. There is a low conversational buzz in the room. Ms. Bouchard addresses confusion as it occurs. The students work steadily and most pairs make it through two problems before the end of the period.

After Reading/Learning

Ms. Bouchard asks for students to contribute tips they have discovered about using the analytic graphic organizer and asks how it helps or does not help when trying to solve this type of word problem. "I like it because it makes me go through the problem step by step and think about it. Otherwise, I sometimes skip stuff," says Robbie. Hannah adds, "I think it makes me more organized, which I guess is the point!" There is good natured laughter as Ms. Bouchard asks students to pick up two blank organizers on their way out the door and to complete problems 4 and 5 for homework.

"Just try them," she says. "See what you can do. We will go over them tomorrow. We will be working on problems like this for the next week so you will get plenty of practice. Good work today!"

Use of *Coding/Comprehension Monitoring* in an Elementary Social Studies Classroom

Mr. Yuan was concerned because he knew that many of his students had scored at somewhat low Lexile levels on the school's reading assessment. Frontloading information and vocabulary before students were asked to read didn't seem to be helping enough. He'd heard from Ms. Carson, a fourth grade teacher, that use of the **Coding/Comprehension Monitoring** strategy helped her struggling readers think about and learn from text. He did a quick online search for some articles and sample lesson plans about Coding, to make sure he knew how to teach this strategy. Then he began to plan his unit on Europeans Exploring America.

Before Reading/Learning

The next day his students seemed mildly curious when they came back from lunch and saw that each American History book had a small stack of brightly colored sticky notes on the top right corner. Once the class settled down, Mr. Yuan opened with a question.

"How many of you have ever sailed or been out in a boat?" Only three students raised their hands. There were very few lakes nearby and most students had never seen the ocean. Mr. Yuan realized they'd need a lot of support to understand the difficulties the Europeans had experienced when they first sailed across to America. "But you know what boats look like, right?" Some students nodded but looked puzzled, wondering what the point was of this discussion.

"Open your book to page 30 and see if the pictures look like any boat you've ever seen." Most students shook their heads when they saw the old-fashioned boats with large masts and sails.

"We're going to read in a different way today and here's what you're going to do. Every time you see something in a picture or in the text that is like something you've personally seen, I want you to mark a sticky note with a check mark. When you see something you've never seen or heard much about before, I want you to place a sticky note right at that line or picture with an X on it. So take your first sticky note and put it by the picture of that sailboat and mark it with a check mark or an X."

He walked around as students placed the notes, seeing that only Tanisha used a check mark. "Tanisha, you've seen this type of boat before?"

"Yes, Mr. Yuan. Last year we went up to Plymouth and they had a big boat there, the Mayflower 2."

Mr. Yuan smiled, "Yes, that's a replica of the one the Pilgrims used. Does anyone know what a replica is?"

"Like a fake?" asked Tim.

"Well, it is not the original. But it is meant to be exactly like the original. So, in a sense, it is a fake. But the purpose is to show as closely as possible what the original was like. So the boat Tanisha saw was a replica of the original Mayflower. Okay! Now here's how I want you to mark text when you read."

Jamie raised his hand. "I know what you're doing, Mr. Yuan," he said. You're teaching us Coding. I already know how."

"Great," responded Mr. Yuan. "Come on up and help me show the others. Anyone else want to help teach Coding with Jamie and me?" Several students shook their heads "no," but Bernard jumped up.

During Reading/Learning

Mr. Yuan explained that today they'd be reading Unit 2, Europeans Explore America. "Would you like to read alone, in pairs, or as a whole class together?" he asked. Most students replied pairs, so he asked them to quickly get re-seated in their pairs. While they all moved, he showed Jamie and Bernard how he had planned to model Coding for the first two pages. "So listen up—Jamie and Bernard are the teachers now."

Jamie began. "Well, I like it. What Coding does is help you pay attention to what you read."

Bernard chimed in, "And it sure helps a lot 'cause you all know I can't read too well and here I am, teaching you!"

Mr. Yuan nodded proudly, noting no one snickered when Bernard admitted he wasn't the best reader. Mr. Yuan constantly emphasized that learning to improve reading requires practice and exercise of the brain, just like learning new sports requires practice and exercise with the body. He was glad that the students seemed to be developing an understanding that hard work and teamwork were keys to learning for all of them.

"And we learned last year that if we watch how someone does it, and then try it ourselves working with a partner or group, then pretty soon we'll be able to do it easily on our own. It's like a trick to make reading easier. So here's how I'd code the first paragraph." Jamie explained how he'd put a sticky note with an X near Columbus' birthplace—Genoa, Italy—and another note with an X next to the line that said "Columbus first traveled to the Canary Islands." Then he showed them how he'd put a note with a check next to the line that said the voyage was filled with danger, especially because of pirates.

"I have a great book on pirates and I know that, even today, there are pirates robbing boats over near the Middle East and Africa." Mr. Yuan chimed in, "I'd put a note with a check on it where it says they were seeking a sea route to China, because my grandparents were Chinese and they have some old trade maps on the walls of their house."

"Now it's your turn," declared Bernard. "You read and code paragraphs 2 and 3, and Jamie and I will come around and help or answer your questions."

Mr. Yuan noticed almost everyone began to read—some silently, some in whispers to their partner. Bernard went over to Andrew, bringing him a book.

"You can put notes on the maps, too."

"On the map?" asked Andrew. "I thought we had to code what we read."

"Sure," said Bernard, "but last year Mrs. Carson told us that you also have to read graphs and pictures cause there's a lot of info there that may not be written out in sentences." Jamie and Bernard walked around helping and nodding as they observed the other students. Students caught on quickly and worked together well. Mr. Yuan wanted Jamie and Bernard to do the reading as well.

"Great job, guys. Why don't you be partners and complete the coding on the reading. Once you finish coding the chapter, you can talk with your partner about where your codes were the same and where they were different—and why."

Twenty minutes later most of the students were still reading and coding with the sticky notes, and Mr. Yuan noticed that two sets of partners were discussing their sticky notes with one another.

After Reading/Learning

"Fine job!" he complimented. "Okay, now I want each pair to turn and talk to another pair of students. Raise your hand every time you find a place where all four of you coded with an X and I will come over and we can talk about it." As the hands began to rise, he moved around the room to see what the common problems were. Vocabulary, he noted, and geographical places. As he listened and responded, Mr. Yuan realized that Coding helped him understand what the students did or didn't understand. This is good for the kids, and good for me, he thought.

"How did you like coding when you read?" Mr. Yuan asked the class.

"It was okay," said Danielle. "I think I understood more."

"I liked it," said Josh. "It made me slow down and pay more attention."

"I'm not sure," responded Renee, "It's kind of different."

"I wanted to know if Carly coded things the same as I did," said Annika.

"I didn't really like it because it made me have to read much slower than I usually do but I guess it made me think more," replied Sam.

"So I think we will do this again with the next chapter but we will add another code: V for new vocabulary," said Mr. Yuan.

"For homework, make a list of the terms and places that you were not familiar with in the reading and write down what you think they mean now that we have talked about them. And think about whether there are other codes that would be worthwhile to use when reading. We can put them up on the board and vote on the ones the class wants to use. Good work today!"

Part 4: Expanding and Deepening Understanding

Part 4: Expanding and Deepening Understanding

Introduction

We know that learning is a social activity, yet we often assign students to complete work in isolation. We also know that to expand and deepen learning, students need to transfer the new knowledge they have developed into new forms. That is, they need to write about it from a different point of view, put it into their own words, create pictures and graphical representations, use specific protocols to talk about, rework, and communicate the content to others. Most students do not find reading and answering questions to be motivating or helpful to their learning of content. In contrast, when students report that when they work in groups, translate content into new formats and apply understanding to new situations they typically find these activities helpful to their learning—and much more fun!

In Part 4 of the Toolkit, you will find a selection of student learning strategies, teacher instructional practices and collaborative routines designed to help students consolidate their reading and learning. Note that this section of the Toolkit has many collaborative routines. Using these regularly in the classroom will promote higher engagement throughout the reading/learning process as they provide an authentic purpose for completing the work.

In this section of the Toolkit, you will find the following approaches to support reading and learning:

	Reading & Learning Phases		
	Before	During	After
Student Learning Strategies			
Role-Audience-Format-Topic (RAFT)	P	✓	✓
Sum It Up	P	✓	✓
Picture This!	P		✓
Collaborative Routines			
Save the Last Word for Me	P	✓	✓
Give One, Get One, Move On	P		✓
Jigsaw	P	✓	✓
Group Summarizing	P	✓	✓
Teacher Practices			
Problematic Situation	P	✓	✓
Classroom Scenarios			
Use of Sum It Up in an Elementary Mathematics Classroom	P	✓	✓
Use of Save the Last Word for Me in a High School English Classroom	P	✓	✓

Note: A **P** indicates the strategy, routine, or practice helps students set a *purpose for reading* and a checkmark indicates the focus of use.

Role-Audience-Format-Topic (RAFT)

Description

This strategy asks students to creatively analyze and synthesize the information from a particular text or texts by taking on a particular role or perspective, defining the target audience, and choosing an appropriate written format to convey their understanding of the content topic (Vandervanter in Adler 1982; Santa, 1988).

Purpose

Use *before*, *during*, and *after* reading to

- Enhance comprehension of main ideas, organization, and point of view
- Process information and reflect
- Provide a creative approach for communicating what was learned that enhances engagement in writing or presentation tasks
- Encourage students to consider perspectives different than their own
- Help students communicate what they have learned using their preferred learning styles

Directions

1. Explain what a **RAFT** is and why it is helpful.
2. Model a **RAFT** for students using a simple text or well-known concept/topic.
3. Assign a text for students to read. Before reading, note the different perspectives in the text.
4. Brainstorm 3-4 possible **RAFTs** students could choose.
5. Asks students to select **RAFTs** to communicate their learning.

RAFT Examples for a Unit on Exercise

Role	Audience	Format	Topic
Newspaper reporter	Readers in the US	Feature	Health habits of U.S. regions
Lawyer	U.S. Supreme Court	Appeal speech	Right not to exercise
Inventor	Patent office	Petition	Revolutionary exercise machine
Heart	Person	Complaint	Not enough exercise
Boss	Employees	Email	Encouraging more exercise

Extensions

- Have students work in cooperative pairs or small groups.
- Have individual students or small groups brainstorm the four **RAFT** components rather than using the teacher-created list.
- Have students present their **RAFT** writing/presentations to other audiences.

Role-Audience-Format-Topic (RAFT) Template

Name _____   Date _____

Concept to be addressed in the **RAFT** _____

Ideas for **RAFTs** related to this concept

ROLE	AUDIENCE	FORMAT	TOPIC

Student's choice for **RAFT** components

Role _____

Audience _____

Format _____

Topic _____

Role-Audience-Format-Topic (RAFT) Content Examples

Mathematics

Have students demonstrate their understanding of geometrical concepts.

Role	Audience	Format	Topic
Architect	Editor of Geometric Homes Journal	Advertisement	2 and 3 dimensional shapes
Student group	School board	Cover letter and design for baseball field	Transformations and symmetry
Toy	Designer	Children instructions for simple puzzles	Geometric shapes

Science

Have students summarize their understanding of potential impact of earthquakes and volcanoes.

Role	Audience	Format	Topic
Research lab scientist	City planning board	Presentation on needed regulations	Probability of earthquake within 20 years
Doomsday religious fanatic	Protest at governor's office	Pamphlets and home video	Recent volcano eruption in state is proof the end is near
Neighbors	Environmental Protection Agency	Petition for insurance coverage	Need for EPA to require insurance for earthquake damage

Social Studies

Help students connect aspects of foreign cultures to their own lives using **RAFTs**.

Role	Audience	Format	Topic
Peace Corp volunteer	U.S. President	Letter and "White Paper"	Increasing US financial support to rural areas
Teacher	Foreign exchange students	Photo-journalism presentations	Literature reflects cultural history and values
Children	Alien from outer space	Discussion	Who they are

English Language Arts

Example for RAFT choices for an essay against teenage drinking.

Role	Audience	Format	Topic
Child	School counselor	Dialogue	Brother's anger and violence when drunk
Homeless teenager	Homeless shelter director	Application essay for housing	How binge drinking caused eviction from parents' home
Parent	Boss	Letter of resignation	Resigning because need to be at home to monitor teenage drinker
Girlfriend	Boyfriend	Series of I-messages	Breaking up because of drinking parties

Sum It Up

Description

This strategy asks readers to select important words that relate to the main ideas of a text reading and to use them in a one- or two-sentence summary. (Reading Quest http://www.readingquest.org/strat/)

Purpose

Use *after* reading to

- Focus students' attention on key words in the reading and how to use them to develop a summary
- Help students develop a process for selecting key words
- Help students use critical thinking to make decisions about what words to include in order to create an effective summary
- Provide an opportunity for students to make choices

Directions

1. Have students read the entire text selection or a designated portion of a text and underline the key words and main ideas, or list them on paper.

2. Distribute the **Sum It Up** template. In pairs or small groups, ask students to share their lists and reach a consensus on what words are important. These main idea words should be listed on the **Sum It Up** template in the space provided.

3. Ask them to write a 1–2 sentence summary of the important ideas of the text, using as many of the main idea words as possible. Together, the sentence(s) may only contain 20 words. Note: Establish up front if articles and conjunctions (and, the) count as words.

4. When each group has completed this activity, ask the group to write their summary on chart paper or the whiteboard. Compare their responses. If students read different portions of the same text, note that some of their sentences could now be put together to create a summary of the important ideas of the text.

Extensions

- Have students create a summary sentence about what they know about the topic before reading the text. After they finish the **Sum It Up** activity, have them compare their knowledge before and after reading.
- Have students complete **Sum It Ups** independently.
- Have students "sum it up" in different numbers of words: 10, 15, and 25.

Sum It Up Template

Name _____   Date _____

Reading selection _____

1. List key words that explain the main ideas of the text.

2. When done, circle the key words that are most important about the text.

_____

3. Using the words you circled, summarize the reading selection in 1–2 sentence(s), together containing only 20 words.

	1.		2.		3.		4.
	5.		6.		7.		8.
	9.		10.		11.		12.
	13.		14.		15.		16.
	17.		18.		19.		20.

Sum It Up Content Examples

Mathematics

Elementary School

In the Everyday Math program, fifth grade students have an integrated portion in each unit called the American Tour. As students read the section, have them use the **Sum It Up** strategy to help them focus on important words related to the main idea and then use these words in a one or two sentence summary. This collaborative routine will promote higher engagement as students read in math class to gain information to solve problems.

Middle School

As students read through the section of the text about circle graphs, have them list key words from the section on a piece of paper. Have students work in pairs or small groups to share and discuss their list of key words. Have students discuss the importance of their word list to the main idea of the section. Ask the students to write a summary of what data are most appropriate to be represented in a circle graph and why.

High School

After students read a section in their algebra book on exponential growth and exponential decay, have them use the **Sum It Up** template to explain a key concept in the text.

Science

Elementary School

To engage upper elementary students in a new science unit about microorganisms, have them read an account from a book or a website about medical mysteries, in which scientists are depicted racing against time to determine the cause and cure for a newly discovered disease. An interesting example is the discovery of Lyme disease, which is caused by a single-celled bacterium that's transmitted by deer tick larvae. Have students work in pairs and use the **Sum It Up** strategy to focus on the key ideas about microorganisms and disease in the story or article they read.

Middle School

While studying about temperature and density, students can read a good summary article or research the internet to find information about various real-world situations in which thermal energy is transferred by means of currents. Examples include convection cells within an enclosed room, in the atmosphere, in the ocean, and under the earth. Model the **Sum It Up** strategy with one article, and then have students use the strategy with the other readings they encounter.

High School

An applied physics curriculum should include links from core science concepts to technological applications in the real world. Assign pairs of students to read different chapters in the book, *To Engineer is Human: the Role of Failure in Successful Design* as a way of demonstrating how engineers use knowledge of science and technology to solve practical problems. Ask student pairs to use the **Sum It Up** strategy to help them develop an effective summary that can be shared in **Jigsaw** fashion with the rest of the class.

Social Studies

Elementary School

After reading a textbook section on geography of South America, have students complete **Sum It Up** to create statements about different countries and about the continent as a whole. Have students compare the summary statements completed at different levels of detail to develop an understanding of how summarizing changes with the topic.

Middle School

After reading a series of letters sent by soldiers during the Civil War, have students use **Sum It Up** to write increasingly brief summaries of what they learned about life during this time. Have students write one sentence using 20 words. Then, have students eliminate 5 words and rewrite the sentence. Compare these sentences and engage students in a discussion about what they kept and what they eliminated.

High School

After reading about and listening to a collection of important presidential speeches, use **Sum It Up** both as a way to have students distill the key messages in the speeches and also to synthesize information across speeches to determine how key themes have stayed the same and have changed over time.

English Language Arts

Elementary School

After reading a picture book as a class, use **Sum It Up** to develop early facility with summarizing. Review each page, asking students to identify the important words. Collect these as a class. Have students vote on whether each word is one of the most important to the text. Finally, have students work in pairs to write a sentence or two that summarizes the book. Share these summaries with the class.

Middle School

During the reading of a whole class novel, use **Sum It Up** at the ends of chapters as a way for students to review the events. Have students work in pairs to list key words, circle the most important ones, and construct their 20 word summaries. Then, at the end of the novel, provide each of these summaries to students and have them develop the collection of summaries they think best summarizes the novel.

High School

During and after reading, use **Sum It Up** to help students summarize complex pieces of writing efficiently. Provide students with practice using this strategy with a wide variety of genres. Have students think aloud the different strategies they use to summarize longer versus shorter texts.

Picture This!

Description

Picture This! is an after-reading comprehension building strategy that helps readers apply higher order thinking skills to their experience as a reader. The strategy asks students to visually represent three to six key scenes or points from a fiction or nonfiction text supported by related captions and text quotes for each picture. It is a versatile strategy that can be adapted for many types of reading assignments and content areas.

Purpose

Use *after* reading to

- Translate ideas from text to image
- Evaluate, summarize, and present evidence/support from the text
- Assess reading comprehension

Directions

- After reading a short piece of text together, select with the class three main points from the story or nonfiction selection. Discuss how each might be represented visually, how each might be captioned, and what quotes from the text best accompany each image. Discuss how the **Picture This!** strategy is another way to create a summary.
- After reading a novel or a longer nonfiction work, ask students (individually, in pairs, or in groups of four or five) to select the three to six most crucial turning points of the novel or critical pieces of information from the nonfiction work. These can be broadly or narrowly defined, depending on the assessment goals for the unit. Have students get their selections approved by the teacher before beginning to draw.
- Ask students to create pictures, diagrams, or images connected to the text. Students should represent details expressed in the text in their visual representations.
- For each picture, students should write a caption explaining what the image depicts. This should be a one to two sentence summary statement of the ideas and importance of each image.
- For each picture, students should select and copy a passage from the text connected to the image's importance in some way. Again, the requirement for the selection of the text will vary according to the assessment goals for the unit.

Extensions

- Use when all students read the same text or when students in pairs or groups read different texts related to the same unit of study.
- Ask students to defend their choices of key events and map students' selections to determine what the students saw as most important.
- Use as a scaffold for analytical writing about a text.
- Use as an assessment strategy when students are reading multiple texts.
- Use as a presentation strategy for **Jigsaw** groups when different texts are read about the same topic.
- Have students take on the role of a text character, author, or personified object when completing the **Picture This!** assignment so they understand how point of view impacts mental imagery.

Picture This! Template

Name _____   Date _____

Reading selection _____

Directions

Evaluate the most important parts of the text selection and picture them in your mind. Draw three to six pictures in the boxes that match your mental image. Give each picture a caption and write a quote from the text that relates to it.

Caption: Quote:	Caption: Quote:
Caption: Quote:	Caption: Quote:
Caption: Quote:	Caption: Quote:

Picture This! Content Examples

English Language Arts

During a study of metaphor and simile, have students identify these in a text and use **Picture This!** to capture the quote and illustrate the simile

Caption: The attackers were like this eagle, fierce, quick, and merciless.

Quote: "The attackers struck like eagles, crook-clawed, hook-beaked, swooping down from a mountain ridge to harry smaller birds..." (from The Odyssey)

Mathematics

After an elementary school lesson or textbook chapter on large numbers, have students identify several comparisons for large numbers and create pictures for those representations.

Caption: A million dollars would be about as long as this football field.

Quote: "One million dollar bills stacked would be roughly 333 feet tall."

Science

During a middle school science unit about "sound," students investigate a variety of noise-making objects and musical instruments, ultimately determining that all things that make sound cause the air to vibrate in some way. After reading about different musical instruments from around the world, and have students use the **Picture This!** template to figure out and then illustrate the special way(s) that each instrument causes the air to vibrate in order to produce sound.

Caption: When the musician blows air, his lips vibrate and the air in the didgeridoo vibrates, too.

Quote: "The didgeridoo is played with continuously vibrating lips to produce the drone."

Picture source: http://blogs.cornell.edu/jennifer/2009/03/10/didgeridoos/

Social Studies

During reading a textbook section on the different structures in local and state government, have students complete a **Picture This!** to describe each function and explain something significant about each.

Caption: The scales illustrate that the judicial branch deals with justice and with making sure that the laws legislators pass are in line with the Constitution.

Quote: "The Supreme Court serves as an important check on the power of the other branches through its power to decide whether laws uphold or violate the principles laid out in the Constitution."

Save the Last Word for Me

Description

This small group discussion protocol supports collaborative discussion of a text. (Developed by Patricia Averette and Daniel Baron.)

Purpose

Use *during* and *after* reading to

- To support students' interaction with text
- To promote reading comprehension
- To clarify and deepen thinking about content

Directions

1. Divide students into groups of three to five. Give each student three index cards.
2. Assign a text to read. Ask students to write quotations they find interesting on one side of the card and why they find each quote interesting on the opposite side of the card.
3. After everyone is finished reading the selection and preparing their cards, the first person in each group shares one of his/her quotes but does not say why this interested him/her.
4. After everyone has taken about one minute to react/respond to the shared quote, the person who chose the quote shares why s/he selected it.
5. Discussion continues in this fashion with each person in the group taking one to three turns as time permits.

Extensions

- Have the group complete a group summary of the text that was read.
- Have the group debrief the session.
- Have each person select a quote to write about in a response journal.
- Ask each group to select the most important quote to share with the class with justification about why it was seen as significant.

Save the Last Word for Me Template

Name _____ Date _____

Title of reading selection_____

Directions: Fill in the three boxes below with quotes that strike you as particularly interesting from the text. Make sure to copy the quote accurately and note the page where the quote is found. Then, below each quote, write why the quote interested you or what it made you think about. Bring the completed template to the meeting with your small group.

First Quote

Pg #____

Reason for selecting this quote

Second Quote

Pg #____

Reason for selecting this quote

Third Quote

Pg #____

Reason for selecting this quote

Save the Last Word for Me Content Examples

English Language Arts

After reading a poetry unit

Have students copy a stanza from a poem onto a card they find interesting with the reason on the reverse side, such as

Archibald MacLeish, *Eleven*

"And summer mornings the mute child, rebellious, Stupid, hating the words, the meanings, hating The Think now, Think, the O but Think! Would leave On tiptoe."—Because it reminds me of how I feel about my mother, always wanting me to keep on studying when school gets out and I just want to be with my friends.

Robert Frost, *Birches*

"But swinging doesn't bend them down to stay As ice storms do."—It gives me advice on recovering from hurt by others.

Mathematics

Before, during, and *after* reading the calculus j-operator unit on imaginary number properties

"The imaginary unit is denoted by the symbol j."—Because my name is Jay and I love science fiction and its imaginary inventions and machines.

"It is impossible to square any real number and have the product equal a negative number. We must define a new number system if we wish to include square roots of negative numbers."—That always made me curious when we worked with square roots before now.

"We need merely to multiply numerator and denominator by the conjugate of the denominator in order to perform this operation."—It's just so funny that the author keeps using adjectives like "merely" to show how easy calculus is and after ten weeks in this course, I still have trouble understanding this book.

Science

During and *after* reading newspaper articles about current science issues

"Fluorescent filaments of the organisms, known as cyanobacteria, began forming in the river last week and by yesterday they streaked the Esplanade lagoons a psychedelic green."—A tiny bacteria caused a major transformation in a short period of time and I wonder how they will get the algae under control.

"Carnoustie, Scotland—Rain was pelting. Sideways, as they say over here. It was a cold rain, too. And the wind? Surely, even the foundation of Glamis Castle had to be shaking."—I picked this as the only part of the paper I really like reading is the Sports section and I enjoy learning how weather affects sports, in this case golf.

Social Studies

During and *after* reading the U.S. Constitution, Articles, and Amendments

"We the people of the United States, in order to form a more perfect Union, establish justice, insure domestic tranquility, provide for the common defense, promote the general welfare, and secure the blessings of liberty to ourselves and our posterity…"—Because it says it all and because I'm worried we're losing ground in achieving this vision.

"The right of citizens of the United States, who are eighteen years of age or older, to vote shall not be denied or abridged by the United States or any state on account of age."—I'll be 18 next year and only at the very end in Amendment 26 is it reflected that youth's ideas are important.

Give One, Get One, Move On

Description

This strategy supports collaborative reflection on, interaction with, or review of a reading selection by using a protocol to solicit responses from multiple readers.

Purpose

Use *before* reading to

- Help students brainstorm key ideas on a topic/reading to activate prior knowledge and build background knowledge

Use *after* reading to

- Help students to summarize and synthesize key concepts in the reading

Directions

1. Set up a box matrix with six or nine boxes and hand out copies.
2. Ask students to write the topic of the template in the topic section. Then ask them to think of an important idea about the topic and write it in the first box.
3. Set up a rotation pattern (e.g., pass to the left) by telling students to pass the sheet to another student.
4. Students read what was written in the first box and write an idea in box 2. It can be the same idea they put in box 1 on their own sheet, as long as it is not the same idea that appears on the sheet that was passed to them. No ideas can be repeated on a paper. If their idea already appears on the paper, the student has to think of another idea to write.
5. Students continue passing on each paper, reading the ideas, and adding new ideas until all the boxes are filled with ideas.
6. Each sheet is returned to the original owner to read and reflect upon.

Extensions

- Use as a summary of different text around the same topic.
- Set up a template to reflect different points of view or different arguments.
- Have students write summaries based on the sheets that they get back.
- Use to generate ways to respond to a text, story ideas for writing, etc.
- Use to help students summarize/reflect on a lecture/presentation.

Give One, Get One, Move On Template

Name _____   Date _____

Directions

Write the topic in the first section. Think of an important idea you have learned today. Write it down in box 1. Pass the sheet to another student who will read silently what was written in the first box. That student will add an idea in box 2. Do not repeat ideas that are already listed. Continue passing on the paper and adding ideas until all the boxes are filled with ideas. Return the sheet to the original owner.

Topic		
1	2	3
4	5	6
7	8	9

Developed by Roz Weizer. Used with permission.

Give One, Get One, Move On Content Examples

Mathematics

Elementary School

After a unit on polygons, pass out a **Give One, Get One, Move On** template, with nine boxes, to each student. Have the students write Polygons in the topic box. Explain to the students the reason for this activity is to help them remember what they had learned during this unit. Ask students to think of an important fact they remember about polygons and record it in the first box. Have students complete the **Give One, Get One, Move On** activity and ask students to pass their templates. Remind students that no idea can be repeated. When the templates make their way back to the original student, have them read over the sheets and write a short explanation of the important facts about polygons from their template.

Middle School

To help students summarize the key concepts taught in an integrated math program, use the **Give One, Get One, Move On** template after each module. Set up a box matrix of six to nine boxes on a sheet of paper. Tell students they will be passing the sheet of paper around to each other to record important concepts they have been studying during the module.

Topic: Module 7 Health and Fitness

Studying sleep data	Using circle graphs	Using line graphs to record calories burned while swimming
Finding heart rate	Understanding capacity	Reading graphs (box and whisker)
Finding volume	Percents	Slope of a line

When every box on the matrix is filled, have the students read over their sheet to remember the important concepts and reflect how the concepts are connected to the module theme.

High School

Before students read the section in their geometry book on geometric probability and area of sectors, have them use the **Give One, Get One, Move On** template to brainstorm what they remember about probability. This strategy will support collaborative reflection and help student review what they have learned in past math classes around probability. This will allow students to activate prior knowledge needed to connect to the new learning of probability and geometric measure.

Science

Elementary School: Habitats

After reading a textbook section on forest habitats, gauge students' understanding of survival needs and habitats by giving them a **Give One, Get One, Move On** template with the recorded topic: "Ways organisms use a pine tree as part of their habitat." Different students should be able to add representative examples, such as animals using the pine seeds for food, or birds using tree cavities for a nesting shelter, or others using the water that collects on the branches.

Middle School

After reading an article or textbook section on different forms of energy, use this strategy to have students consider the types of energy that are at play in different toys, and the energy transformations that make the toys function. Create flow charts to show the transfer and transformation of energy that is happening in each toy and then have students choose one toy to write about, describing the toy, and explaining the energy transformations (including loss of energy to heat). Have students use **Give One, Get One, Move On** template to help them synthesize what they've learned about "energy transformations."

High School

Explore the unifying concept of plate tectonics through reading and hand-on explorations such as map observations (to see the matching shapes of the continents) and demonstrations of the actions that take place at the boundaries between different plates, then read historical accounts of the developing evidence of the mechanisms that explain the movement of continents. Provide students with the **Give One, Get One, Move On** template after reading about all of the lines of evidence, and ask them to fill in the boxes with the different ideas that converged to support this theory.

Social Studies

Elementary School

After learning about the different necessary parts of a community, use **Give One, Get One, Move On** as a way for students to review all those structures. Use the templates as a springboard for extension activities, such as having students describe how the structures are connected or to consider what would happen to a community if one of the structures—such as the fire department—were eliminated.

Middle School

Use this collaborative routine as a way to help students review responsibilities of a citizen in a democracy. **Give One, Get One, Move On** might be used either to have students list different examples of a specific responsibility—voting—or to consider and rank a number of broad areas of responsibility.

High School

After a unit on WWII, use **Give One, Get One, Move On** to have students review the factors that led to the war. Once the templates have all been completed, list the factors on the board/digital display and rank them according to the number of students who have them on their organizer. Then, identify missing factors and ask students to discuss which factors were, according to their learning, the most important and why. Use this as a way to develop students' capacity to synthesize important information.

English Language Arts

Elementary School

At the beginning of the year, activate students' background knowledge and review reading assignments with a **Give One, Get One, Move On** protocol. Using the template, have students list books they read either over the summer or in the prior school year. Once the templates are completed, use them to develop a master list of books students have read, adding to it throughout the year.

Middle School

After a unit on different poetry types, use **Give One, Get One, Move On** to have students review characteristics and features of different types of poetry. Use this collaborative routine either to have students review everything they know about single types of poetry or to have them make statements that capture critical features of multiple types.

High School

During and after reading a novel with substantial symbolism, use **Give One, Get One, Move On** both between sections of a text and after reading to help students synthesize information about symbolism and figurative language. These activities can be collected by students and used for review at the end of the novel.

Jigsaw

[C]

Description

Jigsaw is a group-learning strategy in which students read different portions of a text and then share what they have learned with the small group. It effectively involves all students in a learning task and provides opportunity for differentiated learning (Aronson et al., 1978).

Purpose

Use *during* and *after* reading to

- Involve students in reading and communicating what they have learned with their peers
- Address a wide range of student abilities and interests using reading tasks of differing reading levels, genres, text length, and topics
- Connect different types of reading materials linked to a common theme
- Help students develop reading, listening, and speaking skills and learn from others how to construct and convey important concepts from written text
- Engage students through small group interactions
- Develop understanding about a topic without having every student read every reading selection
- Provide practice in synthesizing information from text and communicating that information to others

Directions

1. Identify what students need to learn from a unit of study and locate from 3 to 6 reading selections that contain the desired content information. Try to vary the reading levels and select high interest materials. To avoid confusion during grouping, mark each selection with a number or color code.
2. Organize students into small, differentiated groups of 3 to 6 members, depending on the number of reading selections.
3. Ask members of the small group to choose one reading selection each. The students will be responsible for reading and then communicating the information they learn to their small group.
4. Explain the **Jigsaw** process to the full class.
5. Reorganize the students, grouping together those who will read the same selection into "Expert Teams."
6. Provide time for each student to read the selection and take notes or create a graphic organizer that identifies the important concepts and supporting details from their reading.
7. In their Expert Teams, members discuss what they have learned and plan how team members will share the information with their small group.
8. Each "expert" returns to the original small group to explain the key concepts of the reading selection to the group members who did not read that selection.
9. In the small group, continue the sharing process until all "experts" have had a chance to share what they learned, and to learn about and note the important ideas in all of the other reading selections.

Extensions

- Use the **Jigsaw** for independent inquiry topics within a general unit of study.
- Have each small group form three or four essential questions to be used for post-assessment of the learning.

Jigsaw Template

Name _____   Date _____

Topic _____

Reading selections used in the **Jigsaw**

1. _____

2. _____

3. _____

4. _____

Notes about selection # _____

Additional notes from other students who also read selection # _____

Student notes about selections not read

\# _____

\# _____

\# _____

\# _____

Jigsaw Content Examples

English Language Arts	Mathematics
After small group reading of four novels on the theme of courage, using Literature Circle discussions	*Before* reading the instructions for the scientific calculator in a Technical Math course
After Literature Circle discussions on the topics below, form **Jigsaw** groups, with one representative for each novel, to compare and contrast.	Activate prior knowledge by having four small groups of students discuss what they already know about one type of calculator features, then break into **Jigsaw** groups for students to lead the review of calculator keys and operations with their peers.
• The author's point of view about courage	• Data entry
• Examples of courageous actions of characters	• Arithmetic operations
• The plot problem, crisis, and denouement about courage	• Special functions
• Examples of how figurative language, symbols, and other literary devices were used to develop the theme of courage	• Combined operations

Science	Social Studies
During and *after* reading text and online materials about the cardiovascular system	*During* and *after* reading about the early Roman world and the expansion of Rome
Form study groups to collaboratively read and research one of the three areas below, then form **Jigsaw** groups after reading is completed for peers to share materials and teach each other the essential components and related vocabulary for each system.	Have students self-select from the following topics for small group research, followed by **Jigsaw** presentations that include information, visual depictions, and links to today's world.
• Blood composition	• The arts of government
• The heart	• Roman life and society
• Vessels and blood circulation	• Roman art and architecture
	• Cicero and Rome
	• Virgil's poetry

Group Summarizing

Description

This strategy supports students to work together to preview text before reading, locate supporting information and examples during reading, summarize their ideas on a four-quadrant chart after reading, and use the notes to scaffold the writing of a group or individual summary.

Purpose

Use *during* and *after* reading to

- Involve students in constructing a meaningful synthesis of what they have read
- Help students learn how to do a summary before they are asked to create their own
- Provide practice in paraphrasing
- Allow students to demonstrate understanding of concepts through the completed group summary chart
- Link the different parts of the reading process
- Develop higher order critical thinking skills

Directions

1. Model the group summary process by preparing an example of a completed chart.
2. Divide students into small groups.
3. Have each student create a four-quadrant chart and label each quadrant with the appropriate topic or concept. Explain that the purpose for reading is to learn important information about each of the topics or concepts they selected.
4. During reading, students jot down notes under each heading with page number references.
5. After students have read the text and make their notes, tell the group to discuss with one another what information and ideas they found that were important about the key words or concepts on the chart.
6. When the group agrees that the supporting information is important, it is added to the chart.
7. Once the charts are finished, ask the group to re-read what they have written and be sure their ideas are clearly expressed.
8. Then have the group collaboratively put the ideas together in a written summary, typically one to three paragraphs, on chart paper so they can share their summaries with other groups.

Extensions

- Ask students to preview the text passage or chapter before reading to identify four major topics or concepts presented by the text author.
- Have students create their charts on the whiteboard or wall poster, so others in the class can see how the ideas of different groups are similar or different.
- Have students use the group summary chart to write individual summaries.

Group Summarizing Template

Name _____   Date _____

Reading selection _____

Directions

- As you read, take notes on your Individual Summary Chart about important information related to the four key topics or ideas. List the paragraph or page numbers next to each note.

- Form small groups to discuss your ideas and come to agreement on important information that should be listed in each of the four key topic/idea quadrants. Add the agreed-upon ideas to the Group Summary Chart. Re-read the final chart to be sure all ideas have been clearly expressed.

- Collaboratively write a group summary, typically one to three paragraphs. When you have finished, copy it onto a large sheet of chart paper so it can be shared with other groups.

Individual Summary Chart

Key topic/idea:	Key topic/idea:
Key topic/idea:	Key topic/idea:

Group Summary Chart

Key topic/idea:	Key topic/idea:
Key topic/idea:	Key topic/idea:

Important! On separate paper, collaboratively write a summary of one to three paragraphs using the group notes. When the group has reviewed and agreed-upon the summary, copy it onto large chart paper so it can be shared with other groups.

Group Summarizing Content Examples

English Language Arts	**Mathematics**
After reading a complex thematic novel, such as *Break with Charity*	*During* and *after* reading a chapter on points, lines, planes, and angles
Formulate four statements for students to respond to in the Individual Summary Chart, then work in groups to agree on summary points based on the novel for the Group Summary Chart, such as	Replace teacher front-loading with group summarizing. Possible postulates to summarize
• The author's point of view regarding peer pressure versus friendship	• Ruler postulate
	• Segment addition postulate
• The meaning of the Salem Witchcraft trials for today's teenagers	• Protractor postulate
• The historical accuracy of this novel	• Angle addition postulate
• Lessons I learned about proving innocence when others perceive a situation differently	
Science	**Social Studies**
During and *after* reading, watching demonstrations, and solving related problems about electrostatics	*During* and *after* reading several civics text chapters about the functions of government
Use group summarizing to review primary concepts for the unit test, such as	Widen students' perspectives about government by having them individually take notes and then check their understanding with their peers about
• Conservation of charge	• Laws and rules
• Coulomb's law	• Distributed, shared, and limited powers
• Charging by friction and contact	• Organization and relationships of national, state, and local government
• Charging by induction	• Operations of the U.S. government under the Constitution

Problematic Situation

Description

This is a strategy whereby teachers introduce a compelling problem or scenario that establishes a purpose for reading to engage student interest and stimulate inquiry (Vacca & Vacca, 1993).

Purpose

Use *during* and *after* reading to

- Motivate students to want to read text and explore ideas
- Make connections to new concepts
- Focus readers on the main ideas presented in text
- Help readers analyze problem/solution relationships
- Ask students to provide supporting evidence

Directions

1. Design a motivating, **Problematic Situation** to stimulate students' interest about important information or concepts in the text material they will read. The situation should be authentic and require analytical or evaluative thinking to resolve. As appropriate, include affective components (e.g., emotions, values) in the "problem."

2. Prior to asking students to read one or more text selections, introduce the **Problematic Situation** and, in cooperative groups, ask them to brainstorm possible results or solutions to the problem. Suggest that each group record their responses and discuss the pros and cons of each solution. Have the groups share their thinking with the whole class.

3. Ask students to read the text selection(s), looking for information that supports their solutions.

4. Ask students to refine or modify their initial solutions as they gain information and evidence from their reading.

5. Ask each group to share their solutions and explain the rationale for their decisions.

Extensions

- Have students locate and use additional sources of information to support solutions.
- Ask students to consider whether some of their own solutions might be preferable to the one presented by the author.
- Use notes and responses as the basis for an analytical or persuasive essay.

Problematic Situations Content Examples

English Language Arts

Assignment: Read *One Flew Over the Cuckoo's Nest* by R. Faggen

The school board has decided to ban this book due to its controversial language and content. Because the principle of the high school believes the book is valuable, she persuaded the school board to take public comments before making its final decision. Since this book is part of our curriculum, the principal has asked you to develop a presentation in support of the text. In order for you to be taken seriously, your presentation must acknowledge the controversial nature of the book as well as the reasons some may think it is inappropriate. What resources and other experts should you reference to persuade the school board? What in this book makes it valuable for people to read? How can you present this information and make a well reasoned argument that the book is worth preserving in the school's curriculum?

Math

Assignment: Chapter on two- and three-dimensional geometric shapes

You have a new part-time job after school at a local architecture firm. Your boss is trying to help you see why math is an important part of architectural design. He shows you the designs for four new homes and asks you to find all of the geometric shapes in the designs and tells you that, by the end of the week, you need to find eight geometric shapes and tell him the name of each shape, describe it, and predict why that shape was chosen over other shapes for that house. Then you are to re-design one part of a house using a different geometric shape and explain why it's a better design for that house.

Science

Assignment: Energy article, http://www.eia.doe.gov/kids/energyfacts/sources/renewable/renewable.html

A company called Northeast Energy recognizes the limited supply of fossil fuels and they have been encouraging their clients to conserve energy. While conservation is an important step, at some point in the not-so-distant future, they realize our supplies of fossil fuels will be depleted and they will be forced to rely completely on alternative energy sources. You have been contracted to evaluate the feasibility of using perpetual and renewable energy sources to provide power for their client, particularly solar, wind, hydroelectric, geothermal, biomass, and nuclear power. They are also interested in any other alternatives to fossil fuels of which you might be aware. What information can you provide that will help them in their future planning?

Social Studies

Assignment: Read chapter 7, "Ratifying the Constitution"

As a newspaper reporter in the late 1780s, you have been asked to write an editorial determining if the process established for ratifying the constitution is fair. The publisher also wants you to discuss whether or not the constitution should be ratified. Based on your knowledge of that time period, what arguments would you include in your editorial?

Use of *Sum It Up* in an Elementary Mathematics Classroom

Students in Mr. Morrison's class often use their fifth grade *Student Reference Book* to find additional information about the mathematics they are learning. Today Mr. Morrison has planned for the students to read a selection that will inform them about the U.S. Decennial Census. The students will use this information as they study how and why census data is collected and demographic trends in the United States.

Before Reading/Learning

Mr. Morrison wrote the word *census* on the board. "Michael can you read the word on the board?"

Michael replies, "Census."

Mr. Morrison then asks the class, "Does this word sound familiar to anyone?" As he looks out at students' puzzled faces, Mr. Morrison asks the students to turn to page 299 in the *Student Reference Book.* "We are about to start a new unit using a specific type of data, census data, collected as far back as 1790. Census data tells us how many people live in the United States. I would like you all to read this page in your reference book silently. As you read, I would like you to write down any key words and important facts/main idea we should know and talk about to better understand how and why the U.S. does a census. Make sure you look at all parts of the page. Once you all have had a chance to read by yourself you will work with a partner and share."

During Reading/Learning

Mr. Morrison circulates and observes as students read and write. Some students finish quickly. "Did you read the notes section and the T graph section?" The students go back and read the sections they missed. "Who needs more time? Are you ready to work with your partners?" Almost all of the students give a thumbs-up.

"Before you start your work, I need to review with you the **Sum It Up** template. If you are not already sitting next to your work partner, move now."

While students were getting situated, Mr. Morrison passes out one copy of the Sum It Up template to each pair. "Please look up here at the screen. You all have received a copy of Sum It Up. I want you first to write the title of the reading selection we just read." Mr. Morrison points to where it says reading selection on the template being projected on the screen, "Right here. Now as you share, with your partner, the key words you have identified I want you to discuss and agree which are the most important words to understand the main idea about the U. S. Census. You will then record these key words here." Mr. Morrison points to the first section on the Sum It Up template. "After you have recorded your list of words, write a one or two sentence summary of the important ideas from what you have read. Try to use as many as of the key words from the list generated. But try to keep your summary to a maximum of twenty words. Does this make sense? Are there any questions?"

Brian raises his hand and asks, "Do short words like *a* and *the* count as part of the twenty words?"

"What do you think class? Should we count articles or conjunctions?"

"Yes," says Brian. His partner Reya nods.

"No, twenty words are not that many to write," replied Jim. Others seem to agree.

"Okay," said Mr. Morrison, "Let's not use articles or conjunctions as part of the word count. You can get started."

As Mr. Morrison moves around the room listening to the students share their list of key words, he is pleased with their discussions. Some students need assistance to get started with their summary. Mr. Morrison reminds the students of the three questions within the article. "If you think about how to answer these questions it should be very helpful as you write your summaries."

After Reading/Learning

"I have put three pieces of chart paper up on the wall around the room. Once you have finished your summaries, I want you to rewrite them on one of the pieces of the chart paper." As the students finish their summaries, they record them on the chart paper. Once the summaries are all up on the chart paper, Mr. Morrison has the student do a carousel around the room to read each pair's summaries. Students move around the room discussing the summaries and what other students wrote compared with what they wrote. Collectively the students show a working understanding on what a census is and how and why it is done.

"Now that you know what a census is and why it is done, we are going to start looking closer at the data collected. We will be looking at the types of questions that have been asked over the years and how they have changed. Does any one have any idea why the census would ask a question about telephones?" Some students start buzzing and others just laughed. The question seems to spark their interest at looking a census data. Mr. Morrison tells the students it is time for lunch and thinks how this is always a fun unit to teach. But he had not tried using the Sum It Up strategy before. It worked well, though, so he is thinking that he will use it again.

Use of *Save the Last Word for Me* in a High School English Classroom

Ms. Snow wondered how she could get her students to engage with poetry. She had read *Abandoned Farmhouse* last April during Poetry Month and thought it might be intriguing to some of the reluctant students as it was short in length, used ordinary language, and had a puzzling ending. She thought it would be a good way to introduce the unit on poetry. She thought she could initially focus on visualization and how poets use language to create powerful lines. But she wanted to get the students talking about the poem. She decided to try **Save the Last Word for Me**, a collaborative discussion strategy another teacher had mentioned.

Before Reading/Learning

Ms. Snow wrote the words *abandoned farmhouse* on the board. She asked students to close their eyes and for 30 seconds form a picture in their minds of an abandoned farmhouse. "Remember to use sensory details to make the image more vivid. What do you see, hear, smell, feel, and taste?" She paused in silence. "Keep that image and find a word that describes the abandoned farmhouse you visualized. We'll do a silent *chalk talk*. For the next two or three minutes, when you see a free piece of chalk, you can go up to the board and write your word. If your word relates to one that has already been written, draw a line that connects them." Students took turns filling the board with words. Afterwards, Ms. Snow asked students to note words they particularly liked and to determine why these words provoked a positive response. Then she solicited student ideas as to what a poem titled *Abandoned Farmhouse* might be about.

Ms. Snow divided a piece of chart paper into four sections and wrote one of these terms in each section: figurative language, imagery, symbolism, and tone. She explained that these words represent techniques poets use to create images in the reader's mind or to prompt feelings in the reader. She asked students if the terms were familiar to them. Several hands went up. "Great. But several of you are not raising your hands and I want to make sure you all know these. So, form a group of three and talk about each of the words and come up with an example. Then have someone in your group come write each of your examples under the correct term on the piece of chart paper. That way we will have a chart for you to refer to throughout the poetry unit. Let's take just 7 minutes to get some examples up." Students pulled chairs together and

discussed examples. There was a lively buzz in the room. Ms. Snow was impressed by the examples that were posted and felt they were a good resource for those who may struggle with the reading.

During Reading/Learning

Ms. Snow projected the first four lines of the poem on the wall. She informed the class that Ted Kooser served as poet laureate for the United States, which is the highest national honor for a living poet. She went on to read the first four lines aloud to the class:

> *Abandoned Farmhouse*, by Ted Kooser
> He was a big man, says the size of his shoes
> on a pile of broken dishes by the house;
> a tall man too, says the length of the bed
> in an upstairs room; and a good, God-fearing man,

Ms. Snow did a **Think-Aloud** to show the class how she read the poem, "Hmmm, I <u>see</u> a big man with big feet and he has talking shoes. Now I am pretty sure that no one has invented talking shoes, so the poet is giving the shoes human qualities. This is an example of personification. I'm wondering why the poet chose to make the shoes and bed talk. That's curious and makes me want to read on. Also, it says the man was a good, God-fearing man and that makes me think he is honest and ethical—that he has good values. That makes me feel like he must be a good person in the way he thinks and the way he acts. Do you see how the language Ted Kooser used helped me to visualize and respond to the poem?" Most students nodded. "Okay let's read the next four lines and this time some of you will share how you interpreted images and responses." Ms. Snow read aloud:

> says the Bible with a broken back
> on the floor below the window, dusty with sun;
> but not a man for farming, say the fields
> cluttered with boulders and the leaky barn.

"Now I need some volunteers—Kara, Dan, Raoul, Mara, bring your chairs up to the front of the room. You are going to help me model the strategy we are going to use with this poem. It's called Save the Last Word for Me. First, I'd like you all to select one line that interests you."

Raoul said, "I like the line 'but not a man for farming, say the fields.'" Ms. Snow stopped Raoul. "Don't say any more; don't tell us why you chose that line. Now

Mara, you have up to one minute to react or respond to this line. Mara thought for a moment. "Why would someone who's not good at farming live on a farm? Why did he become a farmer? Why didn't he fix things like the leaky roof?" Next Dan weighed in. "It seems like they're poor. Is it because the farmer doesn't work hard enough? Or was his tractor broken? Or maybe he was old." After Kara wondered if the guy maybe inherited the farm, it was Raoul's turn again.

"So, Raoul, why did you select the line? You get the last word."

"I like the fields talking part—having the fields talk like they're telling on the guy. Like it's the evidence that he is a guy who isn't a good farmer, but the poet doesn't have to say it. I don't know, I just liked it."

"Okay, good. So how does the poet use language to help you 'see' that image?"

Raoul answered, "I can see fields that have rocks in them instead of crops, and a barn that needs a new roof because it has leaks in it."

Ms. Snow nodded in agreement. "I like the way you noticed Ted Kooser's use of imagery, Raoul. Hearing the group's interpretations of the poem helped me to think it differently."

"Nicely done. Now, in the next part of the class you are all going to use a strategy called Save the Last Word for Me. It is a two part strategy—first you work by yourselves and then you will work with others in a group of four."

"Here's how Part 1 works. I am going to ask you to select two lines from the rest of the poem that strike you as particularly powerful. I want you to pick lines that generate a strong image for you or evoke an emotional reaction. I am going to give each of you a copy of the poem and two index cards. On one side of each card you will write a line that strikes you. On the other, why you find the line powerful—and this could be personal—and then I want you to think about how the author uses language to create the image and jot down a thought about that as well. You might want to use the terms we discussed—figurative language, symbols, imagery, and tone—or you might use the term personification or metaphor—just take a stab at it. No right or wrong here— just some deep thinking about the imagery in two powerful lines that you select—how it strikes you, why it strikes you, and how Ted Kooser, the poet, uses language to make it happen. Note which stanza of the poem contains the lines you selected."

"Now do a good job on these—you will be sharing them in small groups in a few minutes when we do Part 2 of Save the Last Word for Me." The students began to select their lines and write the reasons for their choices.

After Reading/Learning

"Now I'd like you to form groups of four. One person will read one of their quotations and ask others to respond. When they finish, the person who read a quote gets the last word."

Students began working but there was some confusion about the process, so Ms. Snow stopped by several desks and prompted students to only read the quote, not the reason, before the group discussion. Slowly the group discussions began to flow smoothly as students discussed the poem and she noticed that several had selected the same lines.

As Ms. Snow circulated around the room she heard students' thinking out loud. "I think 'and the winter's cold, say the rags in the window frames.' I don't know—for some reason, I can just feel the leaky drafts from the window in that line and it feels sad and lonely to me. I like the image that is created. And the way the rags are talking."

Ms. Snow notes that some of the groups are finished and some are still doing rounds of Save the Last Word for Me. "I am sorry to interrupt those of you who have not finished your rounds of discussion, but I need to give you directions on how to finish up our work before the end of class. The next step is to work together as a group to do a **Quick Write**. You need to identify a note taker to record the thinking of the group. Here are the directions for the Quick Write

1. The group will choose four lines in the poem, one each that exemplifies the ways we spoke about that poets' work with language: figurative language, imagery, symbolism, and tone. The note taker will record the line of the poem and the type of language convention associated with the selected line.

2. The note taker will record the group consensus for the gist of each stanza (1–3) by completing this sentence starter: This stanza was about....

3. The note taker will record the group consensus of what happened to the family by completing this sentence starter: Something went wrong. We think it was... (and tell why)."

As the period ended, Ms. Snow checked in to see how they liked the Save the Last Word for Me discussion and complimented the groups. "You have done some great 'meaning making' and interpretation in your groups. Your discussions of the quotations clearly showed you grasped the author's meaning. So what did you think of this strategy? How did it affect your engagement with the poem or your thinking about what it meant?" A few students shared: "I got a better sense of it when I heard what others think." "It was a lot better than I thought it would be—I hate poetry." "It was okay—I liked that we could write down the lines we liked first."

Ms. Snow compliments the students and tells them they will be using the strategy again the next day with a tougher poem now that they knew how they could work together to have a discussion about a poem. She reminds note takers from each group to put the names of the group members on the Quick Write and turn it in on the way out the door. When reflecting on the class, Ms. Snow thought the level of discussion and engagement for this poem boded well for the poetry unit and she was glad she had tried the collaborative routine.

References

ACT. (2006). *Reading between the lines: What the ACT reveals about college readiness in reading.* Available from http://www.act.org/research/policymakers/reports/reading.html

Adler, M. J. (1982). *The Paideia proposal: An educational manifesto.* New York: Macmillan.

Anders, P. L., & Bos, C. S. (1986). Semantic feature analysis: An interactive strategy for vocabulary development and text comprehension. *Journal of Reading, 29* (7), 610-616.

Aronson, E., Blaney, N., Stephin, C., Sikes, J., & Snapp, M. (1978). *The jigsaw classroom.* Beverly Hills, CA: Sage Publishing Company.

Baron, D., & Averette, P. (n.d.). Save the last word for me. Available from http://www.delmarvaed.org/SaveLastWord.htm

Beck, I. L., McKeown, M. G., Hamilton, R. L., & Kugan, L. (1997). *Questioning the author: An approach for enhancing student engagement with text.* Newark, DE: International Reading Association.

Blachowicz, C. L. Z. (1986). Making connections: Alternatives to the vocabulary notebook. *Journal of Reading, 29,* 643–649.

Buehl, D. (2009). *Classroom strategies for interactive learning* (3rd ed.). Newark, DE: International Reading Association.

Burke, J. (2002). *Reader's handbook: A student guide for reading and learning.* Wilmington, MA: Great Source Education Group, Inc.

Braselton, S., & Decker, C. (1994). Using graphic organizers to improve the reading of mathematics. *Reading Teacher, 48* (3), 276–81.

Carnegie Council on Advancing Adolescent Literacy. (2009). *Time to act: An agenda for advancing adolescent literacy for college and career success.* New York: Carnegie Corporation of New York. Available from http://carnegie.org/publications/search-publications/pub/195/

Carr, E., & Ogle, D. (1987). K-W-L plus: A strategy for comprehension and summarization. *Journal of Reading,* 626-631.

Clarke, J. H. (1991). Using visual organizers to focus on thinking. *Journal of Reading, 34* (7) 526–534.

Cochran, D., & Conklin, J. (with Modin, S.). (2007, February). A new Bloom: Transforming learning. *Learning & Leading with Technology.* Eugene, OR: International Society for Technology in Education.

Council of Chief State School Officers (CCSSO). (n.d.). *Adolescent literacy toolkit.* Available from http://programs.ccsso.org/projects/adolescent_literacy_toolkit/

Duffelmeyer, F. A., & Baum, D. D. (1992). The extended anticipation guide revisited. *Journal of Reading, 35* (8), 654–656.

Duthie, J. (1986). The Web: A powerful tool for teaching and evaluation of the expository essay. *The History and Social Science Teacher, 21,* 232–236.

Fisher, D., Frey N., & Lapp, D. (2009). Meeting AYP in a high-need school: A formative experiment. *Journal of Adolescent & Adult Literacy, 52* (5), 386–396.

Frayer, D., Frederick, W. C., & Klausmeier, H. J. (1969). *A schema for testing the level of cognitive mastery.* Madison, WI: Wisconsin Center for Education Research.

Gillet, J., & Kita, M. J. (1979). Words, kids, and categories. *The Reading Teacher, 32*, 538-542.

Herber, H. (1978). *Teaching reading in the content areas* (2nd ed.). Englewood Cliffs, NJ: Prentice-Hall.

Hyerle, D. (1996). *Visual tools for constructing knowledge*. Alexandria, VA: Association for Supervision and Curriculum Development.

Irvin, J. L., Meltzer, J., & Dukes, M. (2007). *Taking action on adolescent literacy: An implementation guide for school leaders*. Alexandria, VA: Association for Supervision and Curriculum Development (ASCD). Abstract available online: http://www.ascd.org/publications/books/107034.aspx

Irvin, J. L., Meltzer, J., Mickler, M. J., Phillips, M., & Dean, N. (2009). *Meeting the challenge of adolescent literacy: Practical ideas for literacy leaders*. Newark, DE: International Reading Association. Abstract available online: http://www.reading.org/publications/bbv/books/bk689/

Lyman, F. (1981). The responsive classroom discussion: The inclusion of all students. *Mainstreaming Digest.* College Park, MD: University of Maryland.

McEwan, E. (2001). *Raising reading achievement in middle and high schools.* Thousand Oaks, CA: Corwin Press.

Metametrics. *The lexile framework for reading.* Available from http://www.lexile.com/

Pauk, W. (1962). *How to study in college.* Boston, MA: Houghton Mifflin.

Palincsar, A., & Brown, A. (1984). Reciprocal teaching of comprehension-fostering and comprehension-monitoring activities. *Cognition and Instruction, 1*, 117–175.

Raphael, T. E. (1982). Teaching children question-answering strategies. *The Reading Teacher, 36*, 186–191.

Raphael, T. E. (1984). Teaching learners about sources of information for answering comprehension questions. *Journal of Reading, 27*, 303–11.

Reading Quest. *Strategies for Reading Comprehension.* Available from http://www.readingquest.org/strat/

Santa, C. (1988). *Content reading including study systems.* Dubuque, IA: Kendall/Hunt Publishing.

Vacca, R. T., & Vacca, J. L. (1993). Content area reading (4th ed.). New York: HarperCollins.

Wood, K., Lapp, D., Flodd, J. & Taylor, D. B., (2008). *Guiding readers through text: Strategy guides for new times* (2nd ed.). Newark, DE: International Reading Association.

Additional Resources

The following resources are some of our favorites to recommend to teachers of students in grades 4–12 who want to incorporate a strong focus on improving vocabulary development and reading comprehension into content teaching and learning.

Allen, J. (2009) *Inside words: Tools for teaching academic vocabulary, grades 4–12.* Portsmouth, NH: Stenhouse.

Beers, K. (2003). *When kids can't read, what teachers can do: A guide for teachers 6–12.* Portsmouth, NH: Heinemann.

Beers, S., & Howell, L. (2003). *Reading strategies for the content areas.* Alexandria, VA: Association for Supervision and Curriculum Development.

Biancarosa, G., & Snow, C. E. (2004). *Reading next: A vision for action and research in middle and high school literacy*—A report to Carnegie Corporation of New York. Washington, DC: Alliance for Excellent Education.

Bomer, R. (1995). *Time for meaning: Creating literate lives in middle and high school.* Portsmouth, NH: Heinemann.

Buehl, D. (2010). *Classroom strategies for interactive learning* (3rd ed.). Newark, DE: International Reading Association, Inc.

Casner-Lotto, J., & Barrington, L. (2006). *Are they really ready to work?* Employers' perspectives on the basic knowledge and applied skills of new entrants to the 21st century U.S. workforce. Available from http://www.conference-board.org/publications/describe.cfm?id=1218

Ciardiello, A. (2007). *Puzzle them first: Motivating adolescent readers with question-finding.* Newark, DE: International Reading Association, Inc.

Cochran, D., & Conklin, J. (with Modin, S.). (2007, February). A new Bloom: Transforming learning. *Learning & Leading with Technology.* Eugene, OR: International Society for Technology in Education.

Collins, V., Dickson, S., Simmons, D., & Kameenue, E. (2006). Metacognition and its relation to reading comprehension: A synthesis of the research. *NCITE Research Synthesis.* University of Oregon.

Cotton, K. (1991). *Teaching thinking skills.* NW Regional Educational Laboratory Archives. Available from http://www.nwrel.org/scpd/sirs/6/cu11.html

Fielding, A., Schoenbach, R., & Jordan, M. (Eds.). (2003). *Building academic literacy: Lessons from reading apprenticeship classrooms, grades 6–12.* San Francisco: John Wiley & Sons, Inc.

Fisher, D., & Frey, N. (2008). *Improving adolescent literacy: Content area strategies at work* (2nd ed.). Upper Saddle River, NJ: Pearson.

Fisher, D., & Frey, N. (2008). *Better learning through structured teaching: A framework for the gradual release of responsibility.* Alexandria, VA: Association for Supervision and Curriculum Development.

Gallagher, K. (2003). *Reading reasons: Motivational mini-lessons for middle and high school*. Portland, ME: Stenhouse Publishers.

Harmon, J., Wood, K., & Hedrick, W. (2006). *Instructional strategies for teaching content vocabulary, grades 4–12*. Newark, DE: International Reading Association, Inc.

Harvey, S. (1998). *Nonfiction matters*. York, ME: Stenhouse Publishers.

Harvey, S., & Goudvis, A. (2007). *Strategies that work: Teaching comprehension for understanding and engagement* (2nd ed.). York, ME: Stenhouse Publishers.

International Reading Association. *Standards for middle and high school literacy coaches*. Available from http://www.reading.org/resources/issues/reports/coaching.html

International Reading Association Commission on Adolescent Literacy. (1999). *Adolescent literacy: A position statement*. Available from http://www.reading.org/downloads/positions/ps1036_adolescent.pdf

Irvin, J. L., Meltzer, J., & Dukes, M. (2007). *Taking action on adolescent literacy: An implementation guide for school leaders*. Alexandria, VA: Association for Supervision and Curriculum Development (ASCD). Abstract available online: http://www.ascd.org/publications/books/107034.aspx

Irvin, J. L., Meltzer, J., Mickler, M. J., Phillips, M., & Dean, N. (2009). *Meeting the challenge of adolescent literacy: Practical ideas for literacy leaders*. Newark, DE: International Reading Association. Abstract available online: http://www.reading.org/publications/bbv/books/bk689/

Irvin, J., Buehl, D., & Klemp, R. (2007). Reading *and the high school student: Strategies to enhance literacy* (2nd ed.). Boston: Allyn and Bacon.

Irvin, J., Buehl, D., & Radcliffe, B. (2007). *Strategies to enhance literacy and learning in middle school content area classrooms* (3rd ed.). Boston: Allyn and Bacon.

Jetton, T., & Dole, J. (2004). *Adolescent literacy research and practice*. New York: The Guilford Press.

Kamil, M. L. (2003). *Adolescents and literacy: Reading for the 21st century*. Washington, DC: Alliance for Excellent Education.

Keene, E., & Zimmermann, S. (1997). *Mosaic of thought: Teaching comprehension in a reader's workshop*. Portsmouth, NH: Heinemann.

Lattimer, H. (2003). *Thinking through genre: Units of study in reading and writing workshops 4–12*. Portland, ME: Stenhouse Publishers.

Lent, R. C. (2009). *Literacy for real: Reading, thinking, and learning in the content areas* (Language & Literacy Practitioners Bookshelf). New York, NY: Teachers College Press.

Marzano, R. J., Pickering, D., & Pollock, J. E. (2001). *Classroom instruction that works: Research-based strategies for increasing student achievement*. Alexandria, VA: Association for Supervision and Curriculum Development.

Marzano, R., & Pickering, D. (2005). *Building Academic Vocabulary: Teacher's Manual*. Alexandria, VA: Association for Supervision and Curriculum Development.

Meltzer, J., & Hamann, E. (2004). *Meeting the literacy development needs of English language learners through content area instruction.* Providence. RI: Education Alliance at Brown University. Available from http://www.alliance.brown.edu/pubs/adlit/adell_litdv2.pdf

Meltzer, J., & Irvin, J. (2008, Fall). Supporting middle and high school teachers to provide quality content-literacy instruction. *The Exchange, 21* (1), Newsletter of the Secondary Reading Interest Group of the International Reading Association, Inc.

Meltzer, J., & Okashige, S. (2001, November). Supporting adolescent literacy across the content areas. *Perspectives on policy and practice.* Policy Brief series. Providence, RI: The Education Alliance at Brown University. Available online: http://www.alliance.brown.edu/pubs/perspectives/adlitcontent.pdf

Meltzer, J. (with Cook, N., & Clark, H.). (2002). *Adolescent literacy resources: Linking research and practice.* Providence, RI: The Education Alliance at Brown University. Available from http://www.alliance.brown.edu/pubs/adlit/alr_lrp.pdf

Meltzer, J., & Phillips, M. (2008, September). Designing effective content-literacy professional development. *In Perspective* magazine, Ohio Resource Center. Available from http://www.ohiorc.org/adlit/InPerspective/Issue/2008-09/Article/feature.aspx

Moore, D., Alvermann, D., & Hinchman, K. (2000). *Struggling adolescent readers: A collection of teaching strategies.* Newark, DE: International Reading Association, Inc.

National Reading Panel. (2000). *Teaching children to read: An evidence-based assessment of the scientific research literature on reading and its implications for reading instruction.* Washington, DC: National Reading Excellence Initiative.

Ogle, D., & Correa-Kovtun, A. (2010, April). Supporting English-language learners and struggling readers in content literacy with the "partner reading and content, too" routine. *The Reading Teacher, 63* (7), 532–542.

Pearson, P. D., & Gallagher, M. C. (1983). The instruction of reading comprehension. *Contemporary Educational Psychology, 8,* 317–344.

Phillips, M. (2006, June). Literacy: A key link to breakthrough status. [Special Issue] *Principal Leadership, 6* (10), 36–40.

Phillips, M. (2005). *Creating a culture of literacy: A guide for middle and high school principals.* Reston, VA: National Association of Secondary School Principals (NAASP).

Phillips, M. (2003, November). Going for broke: 100% literacy. *Principal Leadership, 4* (3), 22–28.

Plaut, S., Ed. (2009). *The right to literacy in secondary schools: Creating a culture of thinking.* New York, NY: Teachers College Press.

Robb, L. (2003). *Teaching reading in social studies, science, and math: Practical ways to weave comprehension strategies into your content area teaching.* New York: Scholastic Professional Books, Inc.

Roller, C. (1996). *Variability, not disability: Struggling readers in a workshop classroom.* Newark, DE: International Reading Association.

Smith, M. W., & Wilhelm, J. D. (2002). *Reading don't fix no Chevys.* Portsmouth, NH: Heinemann.

Strong, R. W., Silver, H. F., Perini, M. J., & Tuculescu, G. M. (2002). *Reading for academic success: Powerful strategies for struggling, average, and advanced readers, grades 7–12*. Thousand Oaks, CA: Corwin Press.

Tierney, R. J., & Readence, J. E. (2000). *Reading strategies and practices: A compendium* (5th ed.). Needham Heights, MA: Allyn & Bacon.

Tovani, C. (2000). *I read it, but I don't get it: Comprehension strategies for adolescent readers*. Portland, ME: Stenhouse Publishers.

Tovani, C. (2004). *Do I really have to teach reading? Content comprehension, grades 6–12*. Portland, ME: Stenhouse Publishers.

Vacca, R., & Vacca, J. (1999). *Content area reading: Literacy and learning across the curriculum*. NY: Longman.

Wiggins, G., & McTighe, J. (1998). *Understanding by design*. Alexandria, VA: Association for Supervision and Curriculum Development.

Wilhelm, J. (1997). *"You gotta BE the book": Teaching engaged and reflective reading with adolescents*. New York: Teachers College Press.

Wood, K., & Harmon. J. (2001). Strategies for integrating reading and writing in middle and high school classrooms. Westerville, OH: National Middle School Association.

Wood, K. D., Lapp, D., Flood, J., & Taylor, D. B. (2008). *Guiding readers through text: Strategy guides for new times* (2nd ed.). Newark, DE: International reading Association.

Ziemba, S., & Meltzer, J. (2006, September). Getting schoolwide literacy up and running. *Principal Leadership, 6* (1), 21–26.

ABOUT PCG EDUCATION

PCG Education helps schools, school districts, and state departments of education maximize resources, achieve their performance goals, and improve student outcomes. With nearly 25 years of K–12 consulting experience, PCG's expertise, capacity, and scale help educators improve their decision-making processes and achieve measurable results.

Since its founding, PCG Education has offered products and services that help districts and schools achieve equity for all students, accountability for results, and continuous improvement. PCG Education staff draw on a wide range of tools and approaches, including PCG Education-developed models, resources, and software to build systemic capacity through the application of research-based knowledge, sustained professional development, cutting-edge technology, and collaborative partnerships.

As a unit of Public Consulting Group, PCG Education combines expertise in key content areas with a strong set of core competencies to customize services that meet the unique needs of our clients. Our goal is to build the capacity of our clients to improve teaching and learning through data-driven practices, action planning, use of technology, leadership coaching, and professional development.

Direct e-mails to pcgeducation@publicconsultinggroup.com

ABOUT PUBLIC CONSULTING GROUP

Public Consulting Group (PCG) was founded in 1986 as a privately held consulting firm serving state and local health and human services programs. Today, with 750 professionals in 30 offices around the U.S., in Montreal, Quebec, and in Łódź, Poland, our services have expanded to offer a wide range of education and management consulting and technology solutions to help public sector clients achieve their performance goals and better serve populations in need. PCG continuously updates its knowledge of industry best practices and maximizes partnerships and investments to deliver the leading consulting approaches and technologies to the marketplace. The firm is committed to providing proven solutions and outstanding customer service to clients in each of our four practice areas: PCG Education, PCG Health and Human Services, PCG Technology Consulting, and Public Partnerships, LLC (PPL).

On the Web at www.publicconsultinggroup.com